Flying the Hump

飛越駝峰

圖說抗戰期間中美空中運輸

A Photographic History of
Sino-American Air Transport During World War II

主編 / 楊善堯
翻譯 / 廖彥博
作者 / Patrick Hao（郝健坤）、Catherine Liu（劉天悅）、
Ellie Wang（王寶琪）、Everett Wang（王艾唯）、Lucas Yuan（袁浩文）

喆閎人文

目次
Contents

主編序
Editor's Words

This book is a photography album that combines military history, archival images, historical humanities teaching, and international relations between the Republic of China and the United States.

In June 2023, a group of Chinese-American high school students and their parents came to Taiwan under the leadership of Dr. Lin Hsiao-ting, the research fellow from the Hoover Institution of Stanford University. They visited the Presidential Palace, Academia Historica, National Revolutionary Martyrs' Shrine, Chiang Kai-shek Memorial Hall, the Palace Museum, the Grand Hotel, Fu Jen Catholic University, Longshan Temple, Bopiliao Historic Block, Daxi Old Street, and other places with strong "Republican, Chinese, and Taiwanese local culture" style. When they saw these scenic spots, they realized not only the historical and cultural significance behind these sites, but also their connections related to what they learned in the United States and their family backgrounds. This tour gives this group of high school students who came to Taiwan (Republic of China) for the first time a considerable cultural shock. During the visit, they constantly realized that the Republic of China is highly related to the United States where they grew up. This inspired their motivation and interest in exploring this period of history, which was the origin of this book.

Regarding the military cooperation between the Republic of China and the United States in the early twentieth century, it can be traced from the later stages of the War of Resistance against Japanese (1937-1945). When the Chinese government waged a full-scale and arduous warfare, the United States gave China considerable support, from civilian assistance to formal military aids. In the 1950s, while economy of Taiwan gained highly development with the U.S. aids, the military cooperation between the Republic of China and the United States is also a vital part of the Cold War history. The subject of this book, the Hump airlift, is an important part of Sino-American military cooperation.

The five authors of this book, Patrick Hao, Catherine Liu, Ellie Wang, Everett Wang, and Lucas Yuan, use historical photos and archives collected by the Academia Historica of R. O. C., the U.S. National Archives, and the Zhe Hong Humanities Studio to present the subject clearly and richly through chronological arrangement. The impact of visual images is far greater than the feelings that words bring to readers. I hope the publication of this photo album, interpretation of the historical archives by five high school students, will attract more people's attention to this period of history, and help readers understand that historical archives are not only for scholars, even high school students can use them to complete a project.

Yang, Shan-Yao
2024.6.4

這本書是一本結合軍事歷史、檔案影像、歷史人文教學、中華民國與美國國際關係的攝影冊。

　　2023 年 6 月，一群美籍華裔高中生與家長，在史丹佛大學胡佛研究所林孝庭研究員的帶領下來到了臺灣，在總統府、國史館、忠烈祠、中正紀念堂、故宮博物院、圓山飯店、輔仁大學、龍山寺、剝皮寮、大溪老街等地方進行了參訪與交流，這些帶有濃厚「民國風、中華文化、臺灣在地文化」風格的景點，以及這些景點帶來的實體視覺與景點背後所隱含的歷史文化意義，都與他們從小在美國所學以及家庭文化有所關聯，給了這群第一次來到臺灣（中華民國）的高中生們相當大的文化衝擊。在參訪的過程中，他們不斷地發現到一個問題：「中華民國跟他們所生長的美國有著高度關聯性」，這引起了他們去探索這段歷史過往的動機與興趣，也是這本書誕生的緣起。

　　有關中華民國與美國在二十世紀的軍事往來，可從抗日戰爭的中後期開始談起。在中華民國政府進行全面性的艱苦戰爭時，美國從民間援助到正式軍援，給了當時政府相當大的支持，到了 1950 年代後，在美援支持下臺灣快速的全面復甦，尤其在軍事上的援助，更是冷戰時代下中華民國與美國的重要連結。這本書所講述的駝峰運輸這個主題，正好是串聯起這段中華民國與美國友好過往的重要歷史。

　　Patrick Hao（郝健坤）、Catherine Liu（劉天悅）、Ellie Wang（王寶琪）、Everett Wang（王艾唯）、Lucas Yuan（袁浩文）五位作者利用國史館與美國國家檔案館所典藏的歷史照片與檔案，透過照片解讀與時序排列，清楚且豐富的呈現出駝峰運輸這個主題。視覺影像的渲染力與感受力遠大於單純文字給讀者帶來的感受，希望這本攝影冊的面世，透過五位高中生解讀歷史檔案的過程，能引起更多人對於這段歷史的注意，以及讓歷史人文融入應用實作有更多的成果展現。

楊善堯

民國一一三年六月四日

INTRODUCTION

As early as September 1931, China had been under constant pressure from Japan. Following the invasion of Manchuria and the establishment of the Manchukuo puppet state, a military presence allowed Japan to exert control over China's affairs and facilitated potential expansion into the southern regions of China. The Japanese and Chinese militaries engaged in minor skirmishes, building tensions that finally snapped in July 1937 during the Marco Polo Bridge incident. Fighting quickly escalated to a full-scale Japanese invasion of mainland China, setting off the Second Sino-Japanese War and the Pacific Theatre in World War II.

THE SECOND SINO-JAPANESE WAR

While Japanese advances were rapid at first, progress gradually slowed. To the surprise of the confident Japanese commanders, their plan of a three-month war quickly went sour as the Chinese put up strong resistance. When it became evident that the war had dragged on for too long, the Japanese pivoted to a strategy of logistical starvation by seeking to blockade China. By the time they captured Burma in April 1942, the Japanese had successfully closed the main channels of supply to China — shipping through Hong Kong to the port at Guangzhou, shipping through the port at Haiphong in Indochina, and traveling along Burma Road, in that order.

AMERICAN INTEREST IN CHINA

Anticipating the demise of other European colonies in Asia, President Franklin D. Roosevelt strived to keep China in the war to act as a counterbalance to Japanese imperialism while also occupying the attention of a million Japanese soldiers on Chinese soil. Although America sent comparatively fewer troops and supplies to the China-Burma-India (CBI) Theater, America still lent military aid via the Lend-Lease program, signed by Roosevelt in May 1941. The United States later expanded their aid in 1942 when Roosevelt sent Lt. General Joseph W. Stilwell to serve as both the commander of U.S. forces and as Chiang's Chief of Staff.

CHIANG'S INTERESTS AND HIS THREE WARS

To succeed in the CBI Theater, the United States also required the cooperation of Chiang and his Chinese Nationalists. In contrast to the American perspective that viewed the CBI Theater as an extension of the Pacific War against Japan, Chiang regarded the situation as a three-way war. First and foremost, the Nationalists were fighting the Communists. Despite the unity of the Nationalists and Communists against Japan, their civil wars and conflicts of ideology still led to tensions.

The second war was against Japan. For Chiang, fighting the Japanese was a "War of Resistance." The third war prompted the most consideration from the Nationalists — joining the World War II conflict in the Pacific. When he made Chiang the Supreme Allied Commander of the CBI Theater, Roosevelt not only placed Chiang on equal terms with Stalin and Churchill but also burdened him with the expectation to defend India and to regain allied control of Burma.

Without Allied support, Chiang would've lost countless men and territory, if not the war. China had a questionable level of authority from the government in 1941, with a weaker military and an even weaker economy. And after Japan had pushed Great Britain out of Burma, an alternative route was evidently needed.

So Chiang accepted the support but on his own terms. He played other powers off one another, effectively pitting the United States against Japan in the CBI Theater. While he continued to wage small-scale war against Japan, Chiang heavily utilized American support to defend Chongqing while simultaneously making preparations to fight the Communists in the future.

DANGERS OF AIRLIFT

With cooperation in place, the allies decided to establish the first sustained airlift operation in modern history. Known as "The Hump," the operation was located in the southeastern segment of the Himalayas. Supplies would be sent from Assam, India to Kunming, China around the clock, navigating through the dangerous topography regardless of weather conditions. Pilots often only had one hour of rest after completing the 500-mile journey before starting their return. A typical flight to China would take two hours with the support of tailwind, while the flight home could take up to ten as pilots had to fight extreme headwinds while battling to gain altitude.

IMPORTANCE OF THE HUMP

The operation quickly became the symbol of American commitment to China. While initial efforts were primarily symbolic, the operation — which remained the sole artery for supplies to enter China until late 1944 — was quickly proven to be reliable. It was operated by both the U.S .Army Air Force Air Transport Command and China National Air Force, and it also symbolized cooperation between the West and the East. The number of tons per month shipped by the United States through The Hump became a metric to quantify the United States' support for China. Though progress was slow at first, the supplies from The Hump only increased. In December 1942, about 800 tons were supplied by the pilots of The Hump, drastically falling short of the initial target of 5,000 tons a month. But by November 1944, the pilots had surpassed even the ambitious raised target of 10,000 tons a month, and by July 1945, shortly after the war curtains closed in Europe, The Hump had delivered over 71,000 tons in a single month. This commitment served to bolster Chinese national will, achieving the US's goal of keeping them in the war to keep the Japanese occupied.

Without The Hump route, nearly none of the American operations in China would have been possible. Having provided about 80% of the military supply on the Chinese battlefield, cargo dwarfed other supply methods over land via the Stilwell road. Its supplies were directly sent to Major General Claire L. Chennault's Fourteenth Air Force in China, to Lt. General Joseph Stilwell's ground troops, and — though most supplies were directed at the former two — directly to the Chinese government.

AERIAL WARFARE

To the United States, maintaining an air force seemed like the best return on investment compared to infantry or naval alternatives. Thus, the Fourteenth Air Force of America was constituted on March 5, 1943 and formally activated in China five days later. Serving to combat the Japanese, it operated primarily in China, especially in Japanese-held eastern China and Burma. Commanded by Chennault, it conducted effective fighter and bomber operations — including B-29 bombing operations during Operation Matterhorn — and supported the airlift of cargo through The Hump. By the end of the war, the Fourteenth Air Force units destroyed 2,315 Japanese aircraft, 356 bridges, 1,225 locomotives, and 712 railroad cars — while destroying 7.7 enemy planes for every American plane lost in combat by August 1945. Operations were only possible, however, with the supplies of The Hump. Whenever supplies were low, the Fourteenth Air Force had to lie dormant.

Aside from providing the supplies to defeat Japan, The Hump operation was also the proving ground for mass strategic airlift. Although an airlift was not a novel concept, no operation as large as The Hump had previously been implemented. In Europe, airpower was used for bombing, and in the Pacific, it was first used for carrier aviation and later for bombing. But in the CBI Theater, it was used for mass transport along with bombardment. The Hump airlift demonstrated the feasibility of mass air transport and was the inspiration for the Berlin airlift during the Cold War. It also shrunk the globe: emergency supply deliveries that used to take weeks could now be accomplished in mere hours.

緒論

自一九三一年九月以來，中國一直受到來自日本的壓力。日本在入侵滿洲（中國東北）並建立滿洲國之後，得以運用軍事力量干涉中國事務，並進一步向南擴張勢力範圍。此後，中日兩國不斷爆發小規模武裝衝突，緊張局勢升高，最終在一九三七年七月的蘆溝橋事變後爆發，由起初的戰鬥很快升級為日本全面入侵中國大陸，引發第二次中日戰爭以及第二次世界大戰的太平洋戰場。

第二次中日戰爭

　　雖然日軍一開始勢如破竹，但攻勢很快就告趨緩。原本信心十足的日本軍方高層驚訝發現，由於中國的強烈抵抗，致使他們原先設定以三個月時間結束戰事的計畫無從實現。當戰事顯然將曠日持久時，日本便改採封鎖中國的戰略，使中國後勤資源不繼。到了一九四二年四月，日軍佔領緬甸時，日本已經成功封鎖了中國的主要資源補給管道，依次分別是香港到廣州灣的海運、由中南半島海防港輸入的航運，以及沿著緬甸到雲南的公路運輸路線。

美國在華利益

　　美國總統羅斯福 (Franklin D. Roosevelt) 看出，歐洲列強在亞洲的殖民地都將敗亡，因此他竭力支持中國繼續對日作戰，以制衡日本帝國主義，並將百萬日軍牽制在中國戰場。儘管美國派遣到中緬印戰區 (China-Burma-India Theater) 的軍隊和物資相對較少，美方仍然透過羅斯福總統於一九四一年五月簽署的租借法案 (Lend-Lease program) 對華提供軍事援助。到了一九四二年，美國擴大援助規模，並派遣史迪威 (Joseph W. Stilwell) 中將來華，出任駐華美軍司令，兼中國戰區統帥蔣中正的參謀長。

蔣中正的盤算及他的三條戰線

　　為了在中緬印戰區取得成功，美國還需要蔣中正和國民黨的鼎力配合。與美方將中緬印戰區看做是太平洋戰場的延伸的觀點大相逕庭的是，蔣氏認為這是一場三條戰線的戰爭。首先是國民黨與中共之間的爭鬥。雖然目前國共兩黨正合作抗日，但他們的內戰與意識形態的衝突仍使局勢緊張。

　　第二條戰線對抗的是日本。對蔣來說，與日本人作戰是「抗戰」。第三條戰線則最費國民黨思量：加入第二次世界大戰的太平洋戰場。當羅斯福促成蔣中正出任中緬印戰區盟軍統帥時，不但將蔣氏置於與史大林 (Joseph Stalin) 和邱吉爾 (Winston Churchill) 平起平坐的地位，更讓他擔負起保衛印度，以及盟軍反攻緬甸的重責大任。

　　如果沒有盟軍的支持，即使沒有加入中緬印戰區，蔣也會喪失無數兵員、丟失大片領土。一九四一年，中國政府的威信已搖搖欲墜，軍事力量衰弱，經濟惡化更有過之。而在日本將英國勢力趕出緬甸之後，顯然亟需另一條替代路線。

　　因此，蔣氏有條件地接受與盟軍的合作。他在列強之間縱橫捭闔，在中緬印戰區利用美國來對付日本。蔣在國內繼續對日本發動小規模襲擊的同時，大幅仰仗美國保衛戰時首都重慶，並且為將來與共產黨的鬥爭做準備。

空運的危險性

　　駝峰空運很快就成為美國支援中國的具體象徵。雖然一開始時僅止於宣示意義，不過駝峰空運不久之後就證明其確實可靠——一直到一九四四年底，這條空中航線是物資輸入中國的唯一管道。這條航線由美國陸軍航空隊空運司令部和中國空軍共同營運，因此也代表東、西方的攜手合作。美方每個月通過駝峰空運輸送的噸位數字，成為美國支持中國程度的量化指標。雖然起初進展緩慢，但是來自駝峰空運補給卻有增無減。一九四二年十二月，駝峰空運輸送了大約八百噸物資，遠低於當初每個月五千噸的目標。但是到了一九四四年十一月，駝峰航線輸送的物資已然超越每月一萬噸這樣雄心壯志的目標。時間來到一九四五年七月，也就是歐洲戰場結束後不久，駝峰航線每月運量來到七萬一千噸。這項任務增強了中國軍民的抗戰意志，也實現了美國支持中國繼續對日本作戰、以及牽制日軍的戰略目標。

駝峰空運的重要意義

要是沒有駝峰航線，美國幾乎不可能在中國戰場進行任何軍事行動。駝峰航線輸送的軍事物資，占美國援華物資總數的八成，使其他經由史迪威公路進入中國的陸路管道相形見絀。運進中國的物資，直接補給陳納德 (Claire L. Chennault) 少將指揮的美國陸軍第十四航空隊，以及由史迪威中將統領的地面部隊和中國政府——不過大部分的物資，都落在前二者掌握之中。

空中作戰

對美國來說，與陸軍或海軍兵力相比，在中國維持一支空中武力，在投資回報上似乎更為划算。於是，美國陸軍第十四航空隊於一九四三年三月五日成軍，並於五天後正式部署在中國戰場。本部隊任務是在中國對日本軍隊作戰，特別是以中國東部及緬甸日本占領區為作戰地境。第十四航空隊在陳納德指揮下，有效執行空中作戰及轟炸任務，包括以 B-29 轟炸機執行的「馬特霍恩作戰」(Operation Matterhorn)，並且支援駝峰航線的空中運輸任務。到戰爭結束時，第十四航空隊一共擊落了二三一五架日機、炸毀三五六座橋梁、一二二五輛火車及七一二節車廂——至一九四五年八月，美方每損失一架飛機，便能擊毀七點七架敵軍飛機。然而，作戰任務只有在駝峰航線順利運輸補給下才能進行。每當補給延遲時，第十四航空隊就必須暫停行動。

除了提供擊敗日本的物資之外，駝峰航線也是大規模戰略空運的試驗場。儘管空運並不是新概念，但先前從未實施過像駝峰航線這樣大規模的空運行動。在歐洲戰場，空軍用於轟炸，而在太平洋戰場，空中武力首先被運用於艦載機，之後則是轟炸。但在中緬印戰區，它被用於大規模運輸和轟炸。駝峰空運證明了以空運進行大規模運輸是可行的，也是日後冷戰期間柏林空運的構想來源。這條航線也縮短了距離：過去需要數週時間才能送達的緊急物資運輸，現在只要幾個小時即可完成。

**A U.S. B-29 Superfortress bomber parked on the
runway of Chongqing Airport.**

一架美國 B-29「超級堡壘」轟炸機停在
重慶機場的跑道上。

Plane flying over the hump

飛越駝峰的飛機

典藏號 Archive No.：002-120000-00082-179

圖片：國史館 photo courtesy of Academia Historica

Little girl also joined the construction team to build the airport.

小女孩也加入機場修建的行列。

**Heavy bombers of the 14th Air Force refueling
for a long-distance flight.**

第十四航空隊的重轟炸機為長途飛行添加
燃油。

Major Mark Peace, Captain Shao, and the Fifth Army soldiers ready to embark.

國軍第五軍的士兵魚貫登機，美軍馬克・
畢斯少校及國軍邵上尉在旁觀看。

23

September 15, 1944, Yunnanyi Airport: men of the 200th Division in Chiang's National Revolutionary Army taking a transport plane to Baoshan.

一九四四年九月十五日，雲南驛機場，國軍第二百師的士兵正在登機，準備空運前往保山。

**Men inspect bombs to be used in Chennault's 14th
Air Force**

美方人員檢視第十四航空隊將使用的炸彈。

Chennault (middle) with other officers.

陳納德（中）與部屬合影。

圖片：美國國家檔案館 photo courtesy of National Archives

Pilots running toward the iconic e Curtis P40
Warhawk, which stood out for the teeth painted on
the airplanes

飛行員奔向照片中的寇蒂斯 P-40「戰鷹」戰
鬥機，這型飛機以機鼻的醒目塗裝而聞名。

Pilots from the 14th Air Force took a group photo in front of a B-29 bomber in Kunming. They had just completed a bombing mission on Omura City in Nagasaki Prefecture, Japan.

雲南昆明機場。第十四航空隊的 B-29 轟炸機機組人員在座機前合影。他們剛完成了飛赴日本長崎大村市的轟炸任務。

Chinese soldiers are unloading food and ammunition from a C-47 Douglas transport plane of the U.S. 14th Air Force Transport Squadron.

中國士兵正在從美國第十四航空隊運輸中隊的一架 C-47 道格拉斯運輸機上卸下食物和彈藥。

A group of workers preparing to unload an American transport plane that had just landed.

一群搬運工正準備從一架剛降落的美軍運輸機上卸下貨物。

Men prepare a transport plane with supplies before takeoff.

地勤人員在飛機起飛前備妥物資。

General Harry A Halverson, Commander of the 10th Air Force

第十航空隊司令官賀立・哈沃森將軍

Supply transport aircraft stationed at an airport

駐紮在一處機場的美軍運輸機

A man works with welding equipment.
一名技工正在使用焊接設備。

ESTABLISHMENT
OF AIR ROUTE

Following the Japanese bombing of Pearl Harbor on December 7, 1941, the outraged American public spurred the country into war against the Axis Powers of Nazi Germany, fascist Italy, and imperial Japan. Though the United States prioritized fighting in Europe, they maintained their support of China, recognizing its strategic importance in the broader war effort. The United States forged a military alliance with China, providing aid from the U.S. Air Force. The primary objective was to maintain Chinese resistance to Japan, keeping "up to two million" Japanese soldiers occupied on fighting the Chinese — and not elsewhere in the Pacific.

MOTIVATION FOR AN AIRLIFT

Noting the Japanese attempts to blockade supply routes to China, the Allies began their search for potential alternatives. At the time, construction of a new supply route, Ledo Road, had begun in 1942, but due to difficult terrain — mountains, tropical rainforest jungles and swamps, extreme weather — the process would take too long. The commander of the India-China Division of the Air Transport Command, Lt. General William H. Turner, wrote in his memoir that "there was now no other way to get supplies into China except by airplane from the Assam Valley."

During the 1930s, China National Aviation Corporation (CNAC) pioneered air routes over the Himalayas. It became a contractor to operate air cargo services between India and China, and regular passenger flights from Lashio to Kunming. Following the temporary closure of the Burma Road in 1940, the need for an airlift route also became particularly evident to William L. Bond, the operations manager of CNAC. By the end of 1941, Bond and his pilots at the CNAC had developed and mapped out several air routes over the Himalayas. Spanning from the Assam Valley around Dinjan in India to Yunnan Province, centered in Kunming, China, these routes served as alternative supply routes to the road and rail networks in the CBI theater, which were blockaded by Japan.

Bond's team eventually settled on a plan. Planes would transport supplies from northeastern India in the Assam Valley to China's Kunming in the Yunnan Province. Flying over the eastern end of the Himalayan mountains, pilots quickly named it "The Hump." Operations began on April 8, 1942, and was initially tasked with delivering aviation fuel to resupply Lt. Colonel James H. Doolittle's air forces.

THE HUMP AIR ROUTE GEOGRAPHY

The Hump was not just one route. In fact, there were many air routes, separated both laterally and vertically from thirteen bases in India to six in China. The Hump's western terminals were air bases in Assam Valley, while its eastern terminals included airfields in China's Yunnan Province, with Kunming being the primary hub.

During the initial phases of the airlift, the transport pilots had to be wary of lethal Japanese aircraft. Just east of India lay the Japanese-controlled Burma, and Japanese fighters stationed there were ready to shoot down any allied aircraft flying The Hump. The established route was designed to avoid such fighter jets, directing aircraft northward across the Himalayas. But after the Allies repelled the Japanese southward in Burma in May 1944, the route gradually shifted toward the south, where lower mountains and a shorter path sped operations up.

A PERILOUS JOURNEY

Pilots of The Hump navigated through a variety of difficult terrain and biomes, including tropical rainforests, swamps, rivers, and the Himalayas. They took off from airbases in India, starting just 100 feet above sea level. They flew over the Lalmonirhat, Brahmaputra River, Khasi Hills, Naga Hills, and Patkai Range, with peaks exceeding 10,000 feet. Maneuvering through sharp twenty-degree turns over the Upper Chindwin River valley, they ascended the Kumon Mountains, with peaks reaching over 14,000 feet. Following the paths of the West Irrawaddy River, Fort Hertz, East Irrawaddy River, and Salween River, they climbed to 18,000 feet to navigate the Himalayan Mountains, including the Sanstung Mountains (Nu Shan) with peaks between 14,000 and 15,000 feet. Pilots typically flew 3,000 feet higher than these peaks for safety. Descending into the Meigong Rivers, they passed Hengduan Mountains, Dali Mountain, Erhai Lake, and Liang Mountain in China, at an altitude of roughly 6,000 feet to complete the route.

From February through April, The Hump pilots flew the Curtiss C-46 Commando (C-46) and the Douglas C-47 Skytrain (C-47) to navigate the strong southwest winds of up to 100 nautical miles per hour. They had to steer carefully to avoid thunderstorms, which could tower as high as 30,000 feet in the Brahmaputra Valley from May through September. Additionally, the rainy monsoon season between May and September brought the majority of the year's rainfall in a condensed period, with rain persisting for seven to eight hours a day. This resulted in low ceilings and poor visibility, posing further challenges for flying. January's cloudy weather led to a significant rise in icing, turbulence, and snowfall. October through November was in cooler and drier conditions, with clearing skies and reduced intensity of westerly winds along the Hump air route.

CONTRIBUTION AS THE ROUTE OF SUPPLY

In addition to serving as the lifeline for Major General Claire Lee Chennault's Fourteenth Air Force in China and Lt. General Joseph Stilwell's ground troops, The Hump operation also provided other services. It served to transport Chinese troops to the battlefield and wounded American soldiers back to hospitals in India. Ironically, it also provided the United States with raw materials that were abundant in China but short in supply back in America, such as tin and antimony. Other transports included raw recruits from China to India for training and even pig bristles and duck feathers.

The Hump was the sole major supply route to China from 1942 to 1944, before the Ledo Road was finished. It connected China to the outside world and connected all the U.S. military bases in India with those in China. All supplies, munitions, fuel, equipment and personnel destined for Stilwell's U.S. 20thAir Force B-29 Bombers and Chennault's U.S. 14thAir Force fighters for each of their strikes in China, as well as critical war necessities for Chinese troops trapped behind Japanese lines to resist Japanese aggression and troops to defense the Kunming area were flown over The Hump air route.

The Hump air route operation transported Chinese troops, and returned sick and wounded American soldiers to the base hospitals in India, or to Karachi for evacuation to the United States. It also carried strategic war materials such as tin and antimony, which were in short supply in the United States, raw recruits from China to India for training, and even pig bristles and duck feathers. Despite the world's toughest terrain and the extreme weather conditions along the route, the Hump air route facilitated the urgent transportation of bulk logistical supplies, achieving faster delivery and carrying more tonnage by air than what could have been transported via the land route.

Aircraft, air crews, and the increased tonnage carried over the Hump air route became the measure by which the weight of tangible expression of the United States government's commitment to China was gauged. The unprecedented "great military success" achieved over the perilous Hump air route demonstrated the United States' airpower capability to "deliver supplies and soldiers anywhere in the world in a matter of hours" even under the extremely difficult conditions. In Tunner's words, the United States Forces "had developed an expertise in air transportation" and "could fly anything anywhere anytime," "which has paradigmatically altered the shape of modern warfare."

CONSTRUCTION OF U.S. ARMY AIRFIELDS IN CHINA

Chinese armies and the U.S. Air Forces in China required a higher tonnage of supply by air over the Hump to bolster Chinese armies' resistance against the encroaching Japanese forces. In 1943, Roosevelt authorized a plan to supply and deploy B-29 bombers in China, supporting them over the Hump air route from India. The mission was to bomb Japanese industrial targets on the Japanese homeland and in Japanese-occupied territories.

To facilitate the increased airlift of critical supplies over the Hump air route into China, and to support Allied air bombing operations based in China, the Allies launched a campaign to build a series of airfields in China. Chinese workers, under the supervision of the U.S. Army engineers and funded by the U.S. government's lend-lease program, constructed and upgraded three U.S. Army airfield complexes in China using the most basic tools from July 1942 to June 1945.

THREE U.S. ARMY AIRFIELD COMPLEXES IN CHINA

KUNMING AREA

The first complex was located in the Kunming area of Yunnan Province in southwestern China, and included airfields in Chenggong, Changyi, Chuxiong, Yangjie, and Yunnan Yi. These airfields were the eastern terminus of the Hump air route and a key transport hub for Nationalist China. Chinese workers upgraded, expanded, and constructed these airfields from July 1942 to May 1943. They expanded runways to the full length of about 6800 feet(2,900 m) to "give sufficient distance to compensate for the high landing speed of incoming aircraft," and also constructed more taxiways, hardstands and storage facilities at the existing airfields that were initially built in the 1930s.

EASTERN CHINA

The second complex was the repaired and reactivated airfields in eastern China, including airfields in Guilin, Nanning, and Liuzhou in Guangxi Zhuang Autonomous Region; Hengyang, Lingling, and Zijiang in Hunan Province; and Suichuan in Jiangxi Province. Some of these airfields were originally built in 1938 and 1939, and some of them were located behind Japanese lines and served as the front staging bases for the U.S. Army 14th Air Force.

Japanese troops launched massive ground offensives in 1944 in eastern China. To thwart the enemy's plans of utilizing these airfields upon capture, the U.S. Army engineers undertook the painful task of demolishing them, even those recently constructed. In June 1945, Japanese began to evacuate from its conquered territory due to overextension. The U.S. Army 14th Air Force reoccupied airfields in eastern China, overseeing Chinese workers in repairing and reactivating these facilities. They also constructed new taxiways, revetments, fighter strips and support infrastructure. Additionally, they built heavy bomber fields at Suichuan, one of the easternmost U.S. Army air bases in China, as well as at Zijiang, alongside auxiliary airstrips.

CHENGDU AREA

The third complex was located in the Chengdu area in Sichuan Province. It was comprised of four B-29 bomber forward staging bases and three fighter airstrips. The airfield construction and enhancement were finished in only three months, from January to April 1944. Each B-29 bomber runway was built to a length of 8,500 feet and a thickness of 19 inches capable of supporting a seventy-ton aircraft. The fighter strips were built 4,000 feet long, with a thickness from eight to twelve inches. These bomber fields facilitated nine aerial attacks, including four attacks targeting crucial steel mills and aircraft plants on the island of Kyushu, Japan; three strikes on Japanese steel-producing facilities in Manchuria, northeastern China; an attack on an oil refinery in Japanese-occupied Indonesia, and a raid on an aircraft factory in Japanese-colonized Taiwan.

AIRFIELD CONSTRUCTION

ORGANIZATION AND ADMINISTRATION

The U.S. government provided a lend-lease fund to cover the construction cost including the compensation to the Chinese workers. "U.S. Army participation in this gigantic effort was limited to just a few army engineers, most of whom had experience in large building projects." Along with Chinese engineers, a handful of the U.S. Army 14th Air Force civil engineers drafted specifications, prepared layouts, made inspections, and assisted in organizing and administering, and paying the hundreds of thousands of peasant laborers, with no manual labor.

The Chinese Military Engineering Committee controlled the construction projects. Chinese Nationalist local governments recruited 300,000 to 500,000 local workers including women, teens, peasants, and contract workers to work on the airfields. The Chinese workers were organized into groups ranging from 40,000 to 100,000 based on their respective local xian or district. Each xian was allocated a specific section of the airfield to construct and was tasked with ensuring the completion of the assigned work.

URGENCY OF THE CONSTRUCTION

The U.S. Army Air Forces planned to launch their first strategic bombing campaign against Japan, Operation Matterhorn, in the spring of 1944, using B-29 bombers stationed in India to attack Japan from staging facilities in China. The forward staging bases needed to be constructed immediately and made ready by the deadline for this operation.

Additionally, more airfields were required to accommodate the increased volume taken on by The Hump airlift. Chinese troops desperately needed war supplies to sustain their resistance against Japanese forces, and the U.S. Army 14th Air Force needed resources to support aerial combat operations.

To expedite these critical missions, Chinese workers raced against time to construct the U.S. Army airfields. Under a pressing deadline and facing a shortage of mechanical equipment, Chinese workers resided in the rudimentary camps near the construction sites and built four bomber fields and three fighter airstrips in the Chengdu area using primitive hand tools in just three months.

HARSH WORKING CONDITIONS

Before 1945, Chinese workers had to use the most primitive tools and local raw materials to construct airfields. They waded into the nearby and distant rapids and shoals to collect rocks from the riverbed and haul in head-size rocks by "a seemingly endless line of wheelbarrows…to form a foundation sufficient to support the 70-ton bombers." They then spent days breaking rocks into smaller pieces for use as gravels.

Due to the shortage of cement available for constructing adequate concrete runway surfaces, resourceful Chinese workers created a slurry of soil, sand, clay, and water by paddling barefoot in pits. They used this slurry as a binder for succeeding rock layers on the runway. Additionally, they extracted tung oil from local trees and used it as the sealant for the runway surface. After each layer of stone was put in place, they deployed the giant concrete rollers to "pack down the layer of rock and mud slurry."

Chinese workers not only accomplished the airfield construction but also took great personal risk repairing the airfield damage inflicted by Japanese bombings. At Guilin Airfield, for instance, hundreds of Chinese workers swiftly rushed to repair a bombed airstrip immediately after Japanese bombers had departed. In less than two hours, they filled in forty-five craters caused by Japanese bombs.

A substantial sum of money that should have gone to Chinese workers ended up in the pockets of corrupt Chinese Nationalist officials. Chinese workers were paid about 25 Yuan a day (nine U.S. cents), barely enough for food. They were often thin from malnutrition. Despite the material and financial hardships, Chinese workers worked dutifully and tirelessly with their hands, feet, and backs to meet stringent deadlines. Despite the lack of modern mechanical equipment, They not only accomplished wonders by hand with mud and crushed rock, but also modernized and repaired the large network of airfields to ensure the U.S. Army Air Forces attained a high degree of effectiveness against Japanese forces.

CONTRIBUTION AS AN AIR FORCE BASE

Throughout the war, airfields around Kunming played a critical logistical role for China and U.S. military alliance, facilitating the air transport of personnel, equipment, supplies, ammunition, and fuel flown over the Hump into and out of China, as well as across the country. Airfields in eastern China enabled the U.S. Army 14th Air Force to attack the Japanese forces in China. These attacks effectively disrupted Japanese logistics lines, threatened Japanese coastal and river shipping, and challenged Japanese air bases from northern China to Indochina and Thailand. Bomber airfields near the Chengdu area enabled the U.S. 20th Air Force to launch significant offensives against the Japanese homeland after the Japanese bombing of Pearl Harbor. The B-29 bombers made nine raids against targets of Japanese home islands and Japanese occupied territories.

Although the U.S. Army airfields did not stop the Japanese offensive in China, they served as crucial bases that significantly supported the U.S. Army Air Forces. From these bases, the United States provided aerial support to the Chinese armies to combat the Japanese forces, weakened Japanese military capability by striking its vital industrial targets, and disrupted Japanese war logistics. This limited the Japanese troop advances in China and contributed substantially to the overall war effort in China.

POLITICAL SIGNIFICANCE

The U.S. Army airfields in China symbolized the collaboration between China and the United States during World War II. They stand as a testament to the support provided by the United States, and embody the determination, dedication, stamina, and sacrifice of hundreds of thousands of humble and hardworking Chinese construction workers. Furthermore, successful aerial attacks launched from these airfields helped bolster the flagging morale of the Chinese Nationalist forces.

OPERATIONS

Despite its seemingly straightforward path, The Hump route, which stretched from northeastern India to multiple airstrips in China, was anything but easy. The Himalayas contained treacherous peaks and unpredictable weather, and pilots had to navigate through narrow valleys and often flew at extreme altitudes. Even the most experienced pilots fell victim to the Himalayas from time to time. As a result, the combination of high mountains and adverse weather made this route one of the most dangerous in aviation history.

INITIAL OPERATIONS

Pilots and personnel from the U.S. Air Force, Chinese National Air Command, British-Indian Army, and Commonwealth Forces banded together to operate one of the most utilized air transport routes of not only World War II, but all of aviation history. After all, this route was essential to allied success in the China-Burma-India (CBI) Theater. With other resupply routes cut off by the Japanese, the airlift was an invaluable lifeline in achieving American goals in the CBI Theater set by President Franklin D. Roosevelt and General George C. Marshall. They knew that by containing Japanese operations within China, they were successfully biding time for Allied operations in the Pacific Theater.

In February 1942, ten C-53 cargo planes were rerouted from North Africa and sent to New Delhi. Concurrently, airfields began springing up among British fields of Assam and the dense Indian jungle. These departure stations were incredibly dangerous. Newly stationed pilots would recall flying in and seeing black blemishes in and around the runway—places where crews met their end.

While historians debate when operations over The Hump began, most agree that The Hump's operations officially began on April 8, 1942. Lt. Col. William D. Old ferried 8,000 gallons, or 30,000 liters of jet fuel over the Chindwin River Valley, through the Kumon Mountains, and along the Mekong River into China, where it was used to bomb Japan during the Doolittle Raids. This resupply was critical and dealt a lasting blow to Japanese infrastructure. It likewise helped buy time for the allies in the Pacific, supplying Major General Claire Lee Chennault and the famous Flying Tigers to establish a foothold in China against the Japanese.

OPERATIONAL CHALLENGES

Following Old's resupply mission, operations over The Hump continued steadily, but as casualties quickly mounted, morale fell. According to Lt. Gen. William H. Tunner, The Hump became the destination for unruly pilots who were not fit for regular military life. New planes were brought in as pilots perished along the route. According to Air Force logs, three Americans died for every thousand tons of materials flown over The Hump and into China.

In the second half of 1943, a record number of missions were flown over The Hump. The cost, however, was a record number of casualties: 155 accidents and 168 fatalities. Sometimes these accidents were due to human error, but more often it was due to mechanical failure. It was not uncommon for an engine to fail early on in the flight, leaving pilots with one healthy engine and thousands of miles to traverse. Furthermore, due to the extremely high altitude pilots had to fly at, condensation often froze, or "iced up" on the planes. When a plane iced up, the moving parts of the aircraft were more susceptible to failure. Ice could prevent an engine from pumping fuel properly, sending a pilot spiraling down into the mountains below. In an interview with First Coast News, Hump veteran Maj. Herbert A. Songbird recalls when his plane iced up and fell 2,000 feet in the blink of an eye. According to Songbird, they flew their Curtiss C-53's at 17,000 feet, which was 5,000 feet above what their 12,000-foot rating. With the Himalayas towering at 15,000 feet, pilots were often out of their comfort zone and frequently flew with zero visibility. After the pilots made it over the rugged and harsh mountains, they were thrust straight over dense jungle, where Japanese fighter planes could shoot them down. Bailing over the jungle was extremely dangerous. The sheer density meant pilots often got caught in trees. Moreover, these jungles were extremely remote and often inhabited by indigenous tribes. While these tribes attempted to maintain peace and stay out of the war, a Japanese bounty for American GI's meant that pilots and crew who bailed out were often captured and taken hostage. If one was lucky to survive a crash, they were forced to trek all the way back to friendly territory, which could take weeks. All in all, the makeshift planning behind flying The Hump made operations dangerous and rudimentary, as there was a lack of radio towers, proper weather forecasts, and maps of the area. However, there was no other way to mass-deliver supplies into China, where crews such as the Flying Tigers were waging an under-recognized but vital war against the Japanese.

Flying aside, there was a massive drought of spare parts and a substantial lack of competent mechanics, which only further complicated logistics. At one point in time, damaged planes were purged for parts, meaning only four planes were consistently flying The Hump. Moreover, the weather in India created even greater problems. India was extremely hot and humid in the summer with air temperatures consistently at or above 100 degrees Fahrenheit and the airstrip as hot as 130 degrees. During monsoon season, rain and humidity skyrocketed and entire bases were flooded with standing water, prohibiting significant progress on maintenance and repairs. These crude, rushed, airstrips did not host proper hangars, meaning maintenance work often ground to a halt with many crews working overnight to escape the heat, and makeshift bamboo hangars being constructed to avoid the rain. Even though renovations were made, with elevated bamboo pathways being built over areas that flooded, working The Hump route was a nightmare for mechanics who were forced to work with crude tools in foul conditions.

TACKLING DIFFICULTIES

With planes and pilots constantly crashing in 1943, the U.S. military had to find a solution in order to maintain their consistent flying schedule. Their solution was the "Fireball" run. A straight shot from Florida to India, brand new parts and planes were flown from the assembly line to India. An ordering system was even created, with promises of four and a half day delivery from America to India. As more and more planes and parts flooded into these Indian bases, the infrastructure evolved and adapted as well. A ten step assembly line was created, where mechanics efficiently repaired and maintained aircraft in any and all weather. This helped to increase productivity and allowed pilots to get off the ground. However, these efforts would mostly have meant nothing without capable pilots.

The main issue facing The Hump operations was still a lack of qualified pilots. Pilots who survived flying The Hump were often overworked, as most pilots stationed in India flew over 100 hours a month to maintain a steady stream of goods. Additionally, pilots — many of whom had just completed basic training and had never flown twin engine aircraft before — had to fly unwieldy and heavy cargo planes across the Himalayas. According to several accounts, many of the pilots who were sent to fly The Hump were complete novices and would struggle to fly commercial flights under normal conditions.

With inflated casualty rates and damaged morale, another factor that made flying The Hump deadly was the attitude of the pilots. Reportedly, pilots were often so burned out and fatigued that they did not do laundry or maintain proper hygiene. Lt. Gen. William H. Tunner recounts how officers, pilots, and mechanics wore musty uniforms and were not clean shaven. Most pilots assigned to The Hump were only concerned with quickly meeting their flight requirements and then being sent home. Command had set the requirement for pilots at 650 hours, which could be completed in a relatively short time due to the lack of personnel and sheer amount of missions being flown. Coupled with primitive living conditions — tents and bamboo beds — hygiene standards among personnel quickly fell and resulted in the spread of preventable diseases such as malaria and dysentery. Realizing the unsustainability of the current plans, General Tunner attempted to instill discipline into his personnel by raising flight requirements to 750 hours of air time and requiring that personnel be stationed in India for one year before being rotated out. This meant pilots suffered from decreased burnout and operational fatigue, and in turn helped The Hump become a viable and sustainable long-term operation.

SEARCH AND RESCUE OPERATIONS

Another core part of operations within The Hump was search and rescue, as countless flights ended in disaster. Despite slim survival rates, fellow airmen were dedicated to making search and rescue operations successful. Captain John

"Blackie" Porter, was a longtime pilot of The Hump operations who established an innovative and one of a kind rescue service for The Hump known as "Blackie's Gang." Porter assembled a team of experienced and dedicated individuals, including Walter Oswalt, Joe Kramer, and Bill Blossom, to conduct search and rescue. Officially approved by Air Transport Command in October 1943, Blackie's Gang operated out of the action-packed and deadly Chabua airfield with two armed C-47 cargo planes filled with medical supplies, hiking boots, maps, and food. Beginning their missions immediately after a flight was downed or declared missing, Blackie's Gang would tirelessly comb the dense Burmese jungle and steep Himalayas for survivors. They flew at low altitudes and air-dropped supplies and men out of their planes to conduct emergency medical intervention for wounded men. Tragically, Porter met his end when his aircraft was shot down in the Himalayas, and his remains were never found. His search team continued to carry out rescue missions and is credited with saving 127 Allied men and 58 downed planes in their first three months of operations, and were eventually expanded to take care of all search and rescue of The Hump.

PROGRESSION OF OPERATIONS

As the pilots of The Hump found their footing among their dismal living conditions and began hauling more and more cargo across The Hump, the route's usages evolved as well. Major General Claire L. Chennault, who oversaw operations across China, was making progress in the CBI theater and began requesting an increasing amount of supplies. Earlier in the war, Chennault's requests had been relatively meager, and he even sent P-40 planes back to defend the Indian bases that The Hump pilots flew out of. But by 1944, Chennault's demands had expanded, so operations were also forced to expand. As The Hump's tonnage grew, personnel and equipment grew exponentially to match. Air Transport Command increased aircraft counts from 369 to 722. Personnel grew from 26,000 people to over 84,000, and the operation had over 4,400 pilots. From August of 1944 to the end of the war, over 500,000 tons were hauled over The Hump — far surpassing any expectations set during initial phases of operation.

CONCLUSION

The Hump and its corresponding airfields became known as the suppliers of any imaginable wartime goods. Powdered eggs were loaded onto the same plane as bombs. Heating units were loaded onto the same plane as trucks. Anything that could be fastened and broken down that the Flying Tigers and Allied operations needed was put on a plane and sent across the Himalayas. The Hump was one of a kind, and became the most efficient and successful air transport route of the war. The Hump ran 24 hours a day, seven days a week, and only stopped if planes could not take off due to abysmal weather. Pilots who flew The Hump flew over some of the most foul, treacherous terrain in the world, in planes built for lighter loads and better weather. Operations defied logistical challenges as efficiency eventually became so streamlined that planes flying The Hump carried more tons of cargo over a given route than any other aviation operation. Born out of necessity and given primitive technology, gloomy airfields, and undisciplined men, The Hump fueled China during its darkest days of the war, and is the pinnacle of wartime camaraderie and determination. However, the pilots, commanders, and personnel who worked at The Hump do not receive recognition in the modern day. Their stories are overshadowed by those of the men who fought in the Pacific and in Europe.

空中航運
的建立

一九四一年十二月七日，日本偷襲美國珍珠港，憤怒的美國輿論要求美國與納粹德國、法西斯義大利以及日本帝國組成的軸心國開戰。雖然美國將重心擺在歐洲，但仍然支持中國對日作戰，這是因為美方認識到中國在整個戰略大局上的重要性。美國與中國組成軍事同盟，由美國陸軍航空隊提供援助。美國的主要目標是確保中國繼續對日抗戰，讓「多達兩百萬」的日軍被牽制在中國戰場，而不能投入到太平洋其他地方。

空運的動機

　　此時盟軍已注意到日本試圖封鎖中國的對外交通路線，因此開始尋找其他可能的替代方案。當時，一條新的陸路運輸路線，也就是雷多公路（Ledo Road）已於一九四二年開始修築，但是由於諸多因素：山區、熱帶雨林和沼澤以及極端的氣候，使得修路工程曠日費時。威廉‧透納（William H. Turner）中將當時是美國陸軍航空隊空運司令部「印度—中國」師的指揮官，他在回憶錄中寫道：「除了從印度阿薩姆邦河谷（Assam Valley）走空運路線之外，現在沒有其他方法可以將物資運入中國。」

　　一九三〇年代，中國航空公司（簡稱中航）開闢飛越喜馬拉雅山的航線。中航承攬了印度與中國之間的航空貨運業務，並執飛臘戍到昆明的定期客運航班。在滇緬公路於一九四〇年暫時關閉之後，中航的美籍業務經理威廉‧邦德（William L. Bond）明白目前對空運路線的需求變得相當急迫。到了一九四一年底，邦德和他手下的中航飛行員已經開發出幾條飛越喜馬拉雅山的航線，並繪製飛航地圖。這些路線以印度丁詹（Dinjan）周圍的阿薩姆河谷為起點，飛往中國雲南省的省會昆明市，是中緬印戰區的鐵、公路交通運輸被日軍封鎖之後的替代補給路線。

　　邦德的團隊最終制定了運輸方案。飛機搭載物資，由印度東北的阿薩姆谷地飛往中國雲南省的昆明。由於航線飛越喜馬拉雅山脈東端，執行飛航任務的駕駛員很快就將其命名為「駝峰」（The Hump）。「駝峰」空運任務於一九四二年四月八日正式展開，一開始時是為杜立德（James H. Doolittle）中校指揮的機隊提供燃料補給。

駝峰航線地理簡述

　　駝峰航線不只一條路線。實際上，在印度這一端的十三處基地到中國端的六處基地之間，共有橫向與縱向的十三條航線。駝峰航線的西端起點是印度阿薩姆河谷的幾處空軍基地，東端終點站則是遍佈中國雲南的機場，而以昆明為主要樞紐。

　　在空運最初階段，飛行員必須警惕危險的日本戰鬥機。印度東邊的緬甸由日軍控制，駐紮在緬甸的日軍戰鬥機隨時準備擊落任何盟軍飛機。駝峰航線的設立宗旨就是在避開這類戰鬥機，因而引導飛機向北飛越喜馬拉雅山。但是到了一九四四年五月，盟軍由北向南將日軍逐出緬甸以後，航線便逐步向南轉移。新路線飛經的山勢較低，航程較短，任務因而能加快完成。

危機四伏的航程

　　駝峰航線的機隊飛行員必須設法飛越各種艱困的地形與地貌，其中包括雨林、沼澤、河流和喜馬拉雅山脈。他們從海拔高度僅一百英尺（約三十點五公尺）的印度空軍基地起飛，沿途經過拉爾莫尼哈德（Lalmonirhat）、布拉馬普特拉河（Brahmaputra River，中國境內稱雅魯藏布江）、卡西丘陵（Khasi Hills）、那加丘陵（Naga Hills）、帕凱山（Patkai Range），後者高峰海拔超過一萬英呎。他們在欽敦江（Chindwin River）上游河谷處作二十度的銳角大轉彎，上升高度到頂峰海拔一萬四千英呎的枯門嶺山脈（Kumon Mountains），之後沿著伊洛瓦底江（Irrawaddy River）西段、赫茲堡（Fort Hertz）、伊洛瓦底江東段和薩爾溫江（Salween River）的路徑，爬升到一萬八千英尺，飛越喜馬拉雅山脈，包括群峰高度在海拔一萬四千英尺至一萬五千英尺之間的怒山山脈（Sanstung Mountains）。為了安全起見，飛機通常會飛到比群峰還要高三千英尺的高度。接著，他們在湄公河下降高度，通過中國的橫斷山脈、大理山、洱海和涼山，在海拔約六千英尺的航線終點降落。

　　從二月到四月，駝峰航線的機群飛行員駕駛寇帝斯公司 C-46「突擊隊員」(Curtiss C-46 Commando) 和道格拉斯公司 C-47「空中火車」
(Douglas C-47 Skytrain) 兩型運輸機,在陣風時速高達一百海里的強勁
西南風中航行。他們必須提高警覺,以躲避暴風雨,因為在每年五到九
月,雅魯藏布江流域上空的雷雨雲可能高達三萬英呎。此外,五到九月
之間的多雨季風季為全年降雨集中期,每天都有持續七到八個小時的降
雨,導致飛行高度和能見度皆告降低,為飛行帶來更險峻的挑戰。一月
的多雲天候,使得結冰、亂流和降雪等情形顯著增加。十月至十一月氣
候乾燥涼爽,天空晴朗,駝峰航線沿線的西風強度也有所減弱。

駝峰的補給貢獻

　　駝峰航線除了是駐華陳納德將軍第十四航空隊、史迪威地面部隊的
生命線,還有其他功用。本航線空運中國軍隊到前線戰場,並將負傷的
美軍士兵後送至印度的軍醫院治療,或載運到喀拉蚩 (Karachi),準備船
運後送回美國本土。令人感到意外的是,駝峰航線還運送如錫、銻等中
國的豐富礦產,提供給極度欠缺這些重要戰略原料的美國。本航線的其
他運輸項目,包括由中國空運新兵到印度受訓,甚至還有豬鬃和鴨毛等
物資。

　　在雷多公路完工通車之前,駝峰航線是一九四二至四四年間通往中
國的唯一主要補給路線。這條航線將中國和世界連接起來,也將美軍在
印度和中國的軍事基地連接起來。配屬史迪威部隊作戰的美國第二十航
空隊的 B-29 轟炸機群,以及陳納德指揮的第十四航空隊,每次在中國
戰場上發起攻擊所需的一切補給、彈藥、燃料、裝備與人員,都由駝峰
航線補給;此外還有昆明的警備部隊、以及在日軍戰線後方抗戰的中國
軍隊,他們所需用以抵抗日本侵略的關鍵軍需物資,也是由飛越駝峰的
飛機運送的。

　　儘管駝峰航線有著世界上最艱困的地形和氣候條件,卻仍然加速完
成了大宗後勤物資的緊急運輸任務,實現比陸路運輸更加快速的運送速
度和空運噸位。

飛機、機組人員以及駝峰航線增加的噸位，成為衡量美國政府實踐對中國承諾的的衡量標準。在危險的駝峰航線上取得的史無前例的「偉大軍事成功」證明了美國的航空兵實力，代表美國即使處在極其困難的條件下，也能「在數小時內向世界任何地方運送物資和士兵」。用透納的話來說，美國軍隊「已經發展出航空運輸方面的專業知識」並且「可以隨時隨地空運任何物資」，這「從根本上改變了現代戰爭的形態」。

在華美軍機場的建設

中國軍隊和駐華美國空軍需要駝峰航線提供更多噸位的空運補給，用以增強中國軍隊抵禦日軍入侵的能力。一九四三年，羅斯福總統批准了一項在中國部署 B-29 轟炸機的計劃，由印度起飛的駝峰航線為其提供支援補給。B-29 機隊的任務是轟炸日本本土和日本佔領區的工業目標。

為了加快駝峰航線向中國空運重要戰略物資的速度，並支援盟軍在華的空中轟炸作戰任務，盟軍開始在中國建造一系列機場。從一九四二年七月起，至一九四五年六月，美國陸軍工兵團指導中國工人，由美國政府租借計畫提供資助，他們使用最基本的工具，建造並整修了三個美國軍用機場群。

美國在華軍用機場群

（一）昆明地區

第一個機場群位於中國西南方的雲南昆明地區，修築機場的地點包括呈貢、昌邑、楚雄、羊界及雲南驛。這些機場是駝峰航線的東端終點站，也是國民政府統治地區的重要對外交通樞紐。從一九四二年七月起，一直到一九四三年五月，中國工人修築、改善並擴建了這些機場。他們將跑道全長擴建至約六千八百英尺（二千九百公尺），用以「提供足夠的距離來緩衝進場飛機的高著陸速度」，並在一九三〇年代動工修建的原有機場基礎上，增建多條滑行道、停機坪和儲存設施。

（二）華東地區

第二個機場群是在華東地區重新修復啟用的機場，地點包括廣西省（今廣西壯族自治區）的桂林、南寧和柳州，湖南省的衡陽、零陵和芷江，以及江西省的遂川。上述這些機場，有若干於一九三八及三九年開始修建；另有一些機場位於日軍戰線後方，作為美軍第十四航空隊的前線起落機場。

一九四四年，日軍在華東發動大規模攻勢作戰（譯按：即「一號作戰」，中方稱為豫湘桂會戰）。為了防止敵軍攻佔並利用，美軍工兵不得不忍痛爆破這些新近才修築完成的機場。一九四五年六月，日軍因為戰線過度延伸而開始從新占領區撤離。第十四航空隊於是重新佔領華東各機場，並督導中國勞工修復機場設施，以利重新啟用。他們建造了新的滑行道、跑道鋪面、戰鬥機跑道和基礎支援設施。此外，他們還在位於華東最前線的江西遂川機場，以及作為輔助機場的湖南芷江，修建了重型轟炸機基地。

（三）成都地區

第三個機場群位於四川省成都近郊，由四個 B-29 轟炸機基地和三座戰鬥機（驅逐機）機場所組成。一九四四年一月到四月，僅三個月的時間，便完成了機場的修建與強化工程。每一條供 B-29 轟炸機起降的跑道長約八千五百英尺，厚度為十九英寸（約四十八公分），可以承受一架重達七十公噸轟炸機的重量。戰鬥機跑道全長四千英尺，厚度為八至十二英吋。美軍轟炸機從這些機場起飛，完成了九次空襲任務，其中四次針對日本九州重要的煉鋼廠和飛機工廠進行攻擊；日本在滿洲的鋼鐵生產設施遭受三次轟炸；日本佔領下的印尼煉油廠，以及對日本殖民地臺灣的飛機工廠，各進行一次轟炸。

機場建築工程

（一）組織與管理

　　美國政府以租借法案來支應修建機場的成本開支，包括對中國工人的補貼在內。「參與這項龐大建設計畫的美國軍事人員僅限於少數工兵，他們大部分之前都有參與大型建案的經驗。」幾位美軍第十四航空隊的工程師與中國工程師合作，描繪建築草圖、規劃佈局、實地踏勘，並且協助組織和管理數十萬民工、支付民工酬勞，而自己並未實際下場參與工程施作。

　　國民政府兵工署監督修建工程的進行。各縣地方政府招募了包括婦女、青少年、農民和合約工在內的民工，人數約三十萬到五十萬，加入修建機場的工程。民工以縣為單位，編組成四萬至十萬人不等的施工團隊；各縣都被分配機場的特定部分進行建設，並且負責確保完成指定的部分工程。

（二）緊急施工

　　美國陸軍航空隊計畫在一九四四年春天對日本本土發動首波戰略轟炸，也就是代號「馬特霍恩作戰」的任務。本任務預備以駐紮在印度的B-29轟炸機群從中國的基地起飛，轟炸日本。為了任務能如期發動，需要立即進行機場的修建與整備。

　　此外，中方還需要建造更多機場，以容納駝峰航線增加的空運量。中國軍隊迫切地需要後勤補給，以維持對日抗戰；美國陸軍第十四航空隊也需要資源來支持空中作戰任務。

　　為了盡快完成這些重要任務，中國民工和時間賽跑，全力興建美國空軍基地。在工期緊迫、機具設備奇缺的情況下，民工們住在工地附近簡陋的營舍裡，用了僅僅三個月時間，以原始的手工具，在成都近郊修成了四個轟炸機機場和三個驅逐機基地。

（三）艱困的施工條件

一九四五年之前，中國民工只能使用最原始的工具和當地的原料來興建機場。他們徒步跋涉到遠近的激流與淺灘，從河床上收集礫石，用「放眼望去沒有盡頭的獨輪車行列」，推運人頭大小的岩石，「構成足以支撐七十公噸重轟炸機的跑道地基」。之後，民工再以數天時間，將這些岩石搗碎成小塊，用作填充跑道地基的碎石。

由於缺乏適用於飛機跑道鋪面的混凝土，民工們因地制宜，就地取材，他們用腳踩踏，將泥土、沙子、黏土和水在土坑中調製成泥漿。他們將這種泥漿當成跑道填充岩層的接合劑。此外，民工還從當地的樹木裡提煉桐油，作為跑道鋪面的接縫劑。每鋪上一層礫石，工人們都會使用巨型混凝土壓路機，「夯實岩石和泥漿」。

中國民工不但完成機場建設，還冒著巨大的生命危險，修復了因遭日軍轟炸而毀損的機場。例如，在日本空軍轟炸桂林機場之後，數百名工人立即趕往修復被炸毀的機場。不到兩小時，他們就填平了日機轟炸造成的四十五個彈坑。

然而，有一大筆本應支付給中國民工的費用，最終遭到腐敗的國民政府官員中飽私囊。中國工人每天的工資約法幣二十五元（約合九美分），僅能勉強餬口。他們常常因營養不良而消瘦。儘管有如此的物質和經濟困難，民工們仍然克盡職責、努力不懈，在緊迫的期限內完成任務。縱然缺乏現代化的機械設備，但是他們不僅用泥土和碎石創造出奇蹟，更對大型機場群進行了更新和修復，確保美國陸軍航空隊能有效對抗日本空軍。

（四）空軍機場的貢獻

在整個抗日戰爭期間，昆明週邊的機場在中美軍事合作中發揮了關鍵的後勤作用，為越過駝峰進出中國以及全國各地的人員、設備、物資、彈藥和燃料的航空運輸發揮了重大貢獻。華東的機場使美國陸軍第十四航空隊能夠攻擊日軍。這些攻擊有效地擾亂了日本的後勤線，威脅了日本占領區的沿海和內河運輸，並對從華北到印度支那和泰國的日本空軍基地構成威脅。在日本轟炸珍珠港後，成都地區附近的轟炸機機場使美國第二十航空隊能夠對日本本土發動戰略攻擊。B-29 轟炸機對日本本土和日本佔領區的戰略目標一共進行了九次攻擊。

儘管美軍機場並沒有阻止日本對中國的侵略，但它們是為美國陸軍航空隊在華作戰提供大力支援的重要基地。美軍以這些基地對中國軍隊提供空中支援，對抗日本軍隊，透過打擊重要的工業目標來削弱日本的軍事實力，並擾亂日本的戰爭後勤。這遲滯了日本軍隊在中國戰場上的前進，並為中國的抗日戰爭做出了重大貢獻。

（五）重要的政治意義

美國在華修建的機場，是第二次世界大戰期間中美之間的合作象徵。這些機場正是美國支持中國抗戰的證明，體現了數十萬卑微而勤奮的中國建築工人的決心、奉獻、毅力和犧牲。此外，從這些機場成功發動的空襲，有助於提振國軍原先低落的士氣。

飛行任務

儘管駝峰航線看似簡單，但從印度東北部延伸到中國多個機場的航程卻絕非一帆風順。喜馬拉雅山山勢險峻，氣候變化無常，飛行員必須穿越狹窄的山谷，並且經常在極端高度中飛行。即使是最有經驗的飛行員也時常淪為喜馬拉雅山上的亡魂。因此，高山和惡劣天氣的結合，使這條航線成為航空史上最危險的航線。

（一）初期任務

美國陸軍航空隊、隸屬國民政府軍事委員會航空委員會的中國空軍、英印陸軍及大英國協軍隊的一眾飛行員聯合起來，共同執行二次大戰期間、乃至整個航空史上最頻繁的航空運輸任務。畢竟，這條航線對於中緬印戰區的戰局至關緊要。在其他補給路線已遭到日本切斷的情形下，駝峰空運就成為美國在中緬印戰區實現羅斯福總統與馬歇爾（George C. Marshall）將軍所設定戰略目標的寶貴生命線。因為他們深知，透過遏制日軍在中國的進展，便能成功為盟軍在太平洋的作戰行動爭取時間。

一九四二年二月，十架 C-53 運輸機從北非改道飛往印度新德里（New Delhi）。於此同時，英印當局也在阿薩姆邦茂密的叢林裡開闢出一座座飛機起降場。這些起降場極度危險。新進駐的飛行員都記得：當他們駕駛的飛機進場降落時，都會看到跑道旁散布著黑色的斑點——那便是失事機組的殘骸。

儘管歷史學界對於駝峰航線開始運作的時間仍有爭論，不過大多數學者都認為一九四二年四月八日是駝峰正式啟動的日期。由威廉·奧德（William D. Old）中校駕駛的運輸機，搭載八千加侖（即三萬公升）的飛機燃油，飛越欽敦江河谷和枯門嶺山脈，沿著湄公河進入中國。這批燃油，將作為杜立德中校指揮的空襲日本行動的燃料。這次補給行動十分關鍵，因為空襲對日本的基礎設施造成持續性的打擊和破壞，為太平洋戰區的盟軍爭取了時間，也為陳納德少將和他指揮的著名飛虎隊在中國建立對抗日軍的據點提供支援。

（二）任務的挑戰

在奧德成功執行運補任務後，駝峰空運繼續穩定進行，但是隨著失事傷亡人數快速增加，參與任務人員的士氣開始下降。根據空運指揮官威廉·透納中將表示，本航線已經成為那些不守規矩、不適任常規軍事生活的飛行員的派駐地。在機組人員於駝峰航線沿線失事傷亡的同時，新的飛機與人員也持續引進。據航空隊飛航日誌記載：每經由駝峰航線運輸一千噸的物資進入中國，就會造成三名美方人員喪生。

一九四三年下半，飛越駝峰航線的任務次數創下新高。然而，背後的代價卻是創紀錄的傷亡人數：共計出現一五五起飛行事故，造成一六八名人員罹難。這些事故有時是由於人為操作錯誤造成的，但大部分是因為機械故障所致。在早期飛航史上，一具發動機發生故障的情況並不少見，導致飛行員在只剩單具發動機正常運轉的情況下還要繼續飛行數千英里。此外，由於飛機飛行的高度極高，飛機上的管線經常會凍結或「結冰」。當飛機結冰時，負責運轉的零件更容易發生故障。冰霜可能會使得燃料管無法順利向發動機輸送燃料，這就導致飛機失控，螺旋失速往下方的山脈墜落。曾經在駝峰航線執行運輸任務的退役少校賀伯特‧宋伯德 (Herbert A. Songbird) 在接受美國地方電視台「海岸第一新聞」(First Coast News) 採訪時，就回憶當時他駕駛的飛機因機件結冰，瞬間墜落二千英尺的情形。據宋伯德稱，他所駕駛的柯蒂斯 C-53 運輸機飛行高度為一萬七千英尺，比他們一般執行任務的一萬二千英尺高度還高出五千英尺。由於喜馬拉雅山脈高達一萬五千英尺，飛行員經常脫離安全高度，且在能見度為零的情況下飛行。飛行員飛越崎嶇險峻的山脈後，迎面而來的是茂密的叢林，很有可能在此遭日本戰鬥機擊落。機組人員跳傘進密林是極度危險的。叢林樹冠的密度意味著跳傘的飛行員經常被困在樹上。此外，這些叢林位置極其偏遠，時常分布土著部落。雖然這些部落不想生事，也不願招惹戰爭，但日本對美國大兵的懸賞，代表失事逃生的飛行員和機組人員經常被俘虜並被扣為人質。如果機組人員幸運地在墜機事故中倖存，他們只得一路跋涉返回友軍駐地，可能需費時數週時間。總而言之，倉促制定的飛行計劃，再加上機隊與機場缺乏無線電塔、正確的天氣預報和該地區的飛航地圖，使得駝峰運輸任務變得危險和簡陋。然而，除了駝峰航線，沒有其他管道可以向中國大規模運送物資。在中國，飛虎隊等部隊正在與日本人進行一場未被充分重視、但是至關重要的戰爭。

撇開飛行風險不論，備用零件短缺，缺乏合格的機械技工，使得後勤維修工作更形複雜。因為受損的飛機缺乏替換零件，導致有一段時期，駝峰航線上只有區區四架飛機在執行空運任務。除此之外，印度的氣候帶來更嚴峻的挑戰。夏季的印度極其炎熱潮濕，氣溫一直保持在華氏一百度（約攝氏三七點七八度）以上，飛機跑道的溫度更高達華氏一百三十度。在季風季節，降雨和濕度急遽上升，機場嚴重積水，妨礙維護與修理作業的進行。這些因陋就簡、倉促完工的機場往往沒有像樣的機棚，地勤維修工作因此時常陷入停頓。許多機組人員徹夜通宵工作，以避開日間酷熱，而且還須搭建竹製機棚，使飛機免受雨淋。儘管這些機場多次進行整建翻修，在易受洪水氾濫的地點搭建了竹架通行步道，可是對於在這樣艱困環境下使用簡陋器具進行維修的技師來說，在駝峰航線服役真是噩夢一場。

（三）克服難關

由於一九四三年時頻繁發生墜機事故，造成諸多飛機與機組人員傷亡，美國軍方必須找出解決方案，以維持空運計畫的進行。軍方提出的解決方案，是所謂「火球」配送方案（Fireball run）：全新的飛機和機組零件，從佛羅里達州的裝配線直接空運到印度。軍方甚至還為此設置了一套訂單程序，承諾只需四天半的時間，就可以將物件從美國送抵印度。隨著越來越多的飛機和機組零件抵達這些印度基地，基礎設施也跟著不斷發展和調整。基地創設了「十步驟裝配線」（ten step assembly line），使機械技師可以在任何氣候條件下有效修理和維護飛機。這些措施都有助於生產力的提升，並使得飛行員得以駕駛飛機升空執行任務。然而，要是缺乏稱職的飛行員，上述的努力都將毫無意義。

駝峰航線面臨的主要問題仍然是欠缺合格的飛行員。能夠勝任駝峰航線飛行任務的駕駛員時常過度勞累。由於需要維持穩定的空運量，大多數駐紮在印度的飛行員每月飛行時數都在一百小時以上。此外，飛行員（其中許多人剛完成基礎訓練，而且此前從未駕駛過雙引擎飛機）不得不駕駛笨重的大型貨機飛越喜馬拉雅山。據若干文獻的說法，許多被派去駝峰航線的飛行員都是初出茅廬的新手，原本在正常條件下很難執飛商業航班。

除了傷亡率居高不下、機組人員士氣低落之外，致使駝峰成為「死亡航線」的另一個因素，正是飛行員的態度。據稱，飛行員時常精疲力竭，衣服不得換洗，個人衛生也無法保持。在指揮官威廉・透納中將的回憶裡，就有描述軍官、飛行員和機工技師們穿著霉臭的制服、滿面鬍渣的情景。多數派駐駝峰航線的飛行員，一心只想儘速滿足飛行時數規定，然後趕快調派回國。指揮部將飛行時數的需求訂在六百五十小時，由於人員缺乏而任務量龐大，這項需求可以在相對較短的時間內完成。不但如此，再加上居住環境極其原始（帳篷與竹床），導致人員的健康情況急遽下降，瘧疾、痢疾等原本可預防的疾病開始傳播。透納中將意識到如若長此以往，將無法持續進行目前的任務，於是試圖向部屬申明紀律，先是將任務飛行時數要求提高到七百五十小時，並規定派駐印度人員需滿一年才能申請輪調。這些措施使飛行員的倦怠和執行任務的疲勞有所減輕，從而讓駝峰航線得以可長可久的運作下去。

（四）搜救任務

由於空難事故頻傳，搜救行動是駝峰航線的另一個核心任務。雖然失事人員的生還率很低，但飛行員還是努力搜救同袍。約翰‧「布萊基」‧波特 (John "Blackie" Porter) 上尉是長期服役於駝峰航線的飛行員，他開創了一種全新且獨特的救援模式，其團隊被稱為「布萊基幫」(Blackie's Gang)。波特的搜救隊員經驗豐富，且充滿熱誠，有華特‧奧斯華（Walter Oswalt）、喬‧克拉瑪 (Joe Kramer) 和比爾‧布隆森 (Bill Blossom) 等好手在列。一九四三年十月，航空運輸指揮部正式批准，撥給「布萊基幫」兩架載有醫療用品、登山器材、地圖和口糧的 C-47 武裝貨機，派駐在任務繁重又事故頻傳的查布阿 (Chabua) 機場待命。每當有飛機遭到擊落或是宣告失蹤，「布萊基幫」就立即展開搜救任務，他們不知疲倦地在茂密的緬甸叢林和陡峭的喜馬拉雅山中搜尋生還者。搜救飛機低空飛行，空投物資和人員，為傷者進行緊急醫療處置。不幸的是，波特的座機在喜馬拉雅山區被擊落，波特罹難，遺體至今未能尋獲。他成立的搜救小隊繼續執行救援任務，在展開任務的前三個月就拯救了一二七名盟軍人員和五十八架墜毀的飛機。最終，他們負責搜救的範圍，擴大到整個駝峰航線。

任務進展

隨著駝峰航線的飛行員在惡劣的生活條件中站穩腳跟，並逐步運送越來越多的物資，這條航線的用途也發生了變化。負責督導中國各地作戰任務的陳納德少將在 中緬印戰區取得進展，於是他開始要求增加物資供應量。戰爭初期，陳納德的物資需求相對較少，他甚至還派出麾下的 P-40 驅逐機返航保衛駝峰飛行員起飛的印度基地。但到了一九四四年，陳納德的需求擴大了，因此駝峰的運輸業務也跟著擴大。隨著駝峰噸位的增加，人員和設備也隨之呈指數級增長。航空運輸司令部將飛機數量從三六九架增加到七二二架。從一九四四年八月到戰爭結束，駝峰航線的運輸量超過五十萬噸，遠遠超出了任務開展初期所設定的一切預期。

結論

　　駝峰航線及其出發端的機場可以供應任何可以想像的戰時物資。雞蛋粉 (powdered eggs，將蛋液乾燥製成粉狀的戰時口糧) 與炸彈、暖氣設備與卡車，都能裝載在同一架飛機上運送。任何可以綁緊固定和分解的物件，只要是飛虎隊和盟軍作戰任務所需，全都被裝上飛機飛越喜馬拉雅山。駝峰航線是獨一無二的空運路線，而且是二次大戰中最有效、最成功的航空運輸路線。駝峰航線每週七天、每天二十四小時持續運作，只有在天氣極度惡劣、飛機無法起飛時才會暫時停止。駝峰航線的飛行員，駕駛著搭載量超過設計載重的飛機，經歷超出機體所能承受的惡劣天候，飛越了世界上最惡劣、最危險的地形。航線的營運克服了後勤挑戰，因為最終作業流程變得如此精簡有效率，以至於飛行駝峰航線的飛機在特定航線上運載的貨物比任何其他航空運營都還來得多。

　　因應戰局需求，駝峰航線應運而生。在技術落後、機場簡陋、人員紀律蕩然等不利條件之下，駝峰航線在中國對日戰爭最黑暗的時期，提供了重要的物資，是戰時中美友誼與決心的頂峰。然而，服役於駝峰航線的飛行員、指揮官和地勤人員並沒有得到當代的重視。他們的故事被太平洋和歐洲的戰爭事蹟所掩蓋。

The Hump was established when the first cargo-carrying flight over The Hump flew in April 1942, hauling gasoline for the Doolittle Raiders. This photo shows Kunming Airfield, where people are curiously watching B-29 bomber Dauntless Dottie and its pilot, who have just returned after bombing Omura City in Nagasaki Prefecture, Japan.

一九四二年四月，第一架貨機飛越駝峰航線，為杜立特空襲日本的機隊運輸汽油，駝峰航線由此開始。圖為昆明機場，人們好奇地觀看轟炸日本長崎縣大村市後剛返航的 B-29 轟炸機「無畏多蒂」及其飛行員。

Troops unloading cargo from a plane that just flew The Hump.

部隊從剛飛越駝峰航線的飛機上卸下貨物。

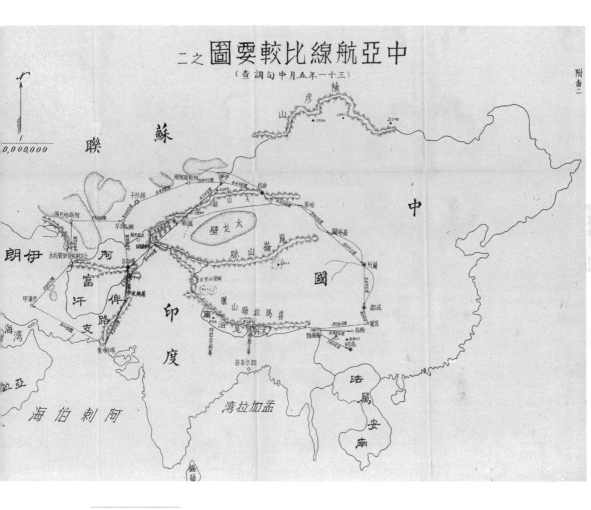

Map of Air Route Comparisons in Central Asia operated by China National Aviation Corp. (Survey conducted in mid-May, 1942)

中亞航線比較要圖（一九四二年五月中旬調查繪製）。

Map of Airfield Distribution in Southern China and Northwestern India, developed in response to China's then external transportation challenges and supply shortages at that time.

「南疆機場設施及印度西北部機場狀況圖」
（一九四二年六月上旬調查繪製）

American and Chinese soldiers in Northern Burma load boxes of ammunition aboard river boats to move them to frontline positions where Chinese and American forces are engaged in fighting the Japanese. Following the Japanese occupation of Burma, essential supplies and equipment for the Allied forces in the Burma theater are airlifted by planes of the U.S. Army Air Transport Command via the Hump air route.

緬北的美軍和中國士兵將一箱箱彈藥裝上河船，運往中美軍隊與日軍作戰的前線陣地。日本佔領緬甸後，緬甸戰區盟軍的必需物資和設備，必須由美國陸軍航空運輸司令部的飛機飛越駝峰航線空運。

Railway at an airfield for the Hump airlift

為了運載駝峰航線物資而修築的機場鐵路。

圖片：美國國家檔案館 photo courtesy of National Archives

THE FLYING
TIGERS

Formed in response to the need to fight against Japanese aggression during World War II, the Fourteenth Air Force was established on March 5, 1943 as a pivotal force in the conflict, playing a crucial role in the Allied efforts against Axis powers in the China-Burma-India (CBI) Theater. It was composed by a team of highly experienced pilots, many of whom were veterans of other theaters of the war. But prior to its creation, there was another unit, composed of approximately 300 volunteer pilots, known as the American Volunteer Group (AVG).

The AVG was launched into action in 1941 and disbanded in 1942, whereupon many of the personnel associated with the Flying Tigers were absorbed into the newly established Fourteenth Air Force, which was activated in 1943, under the command of Major General Claire L. Chennault.

AVG's aircrafts stood out due to its appearance: a distinctive shark's mouth paint scheme at the nose of each plane. The shark's teeth were intended to strike as an intimidation tactic by making the aircraft appear more aggressive and predatory. It also served as an effective way to differentiate between the multitude of aircraft, allowing both friendly and enemy forces to recognize the unit quickly in the chaos of aerial combat. But most importantly, it provided a sense of camaraderie between the AVG pilots — a symbol of pride and solidarity. The unique paint scheme also earned the AVG the moniker 'Flying Tigers.'

MAJOR GENERAL CLAIRE L. CHENNAULT

Chennault was undeniably an outstanding leader for both the Flying Tigers and the Fourteenth Air Force, showing an aptitude for flying from an early age. He learned to fly during World War I after joining the U.S. Army Air Corps in 1917. He was appointed to China shortly after the start of the Sino-Japanese war with hopes of assisting China and the rest of the Allied powers.

Prior to his time at Fourteenth Air Force, he was already respected for his expertise in aerial combat and was credited with several victories during his time working in China. As the founder and leader of the AVG, he was a man renowned for his effective leadership and tactical innovations. He emphasized aggressive tactics, flexibility, and cooperation with Chinese forces, all of which contributed greatly to the unit's success.

In particular, Chennault was an advocate for defensive tactics—strategies aimed at preventing unnecessary harm from befalling pilots—believing that defensive tactics were equally as important as combatant methods in aerial combat. He promoted the use of "hit-and-run" strategies, which involved surprising enemy aircraft from a higher altitude with diving attacks, then quickly climbing away to avoid counterattacks, which allowed the Flying Tigers to capitalize on their aircraft's speed and firepower while minimizing exposure to enemy fire.

Chennault's unit also utilized the Thach Weave Maneuver tactic, designed as a defensive technique to counter the superior Japanese aircraft Zero-sen. It ensured that two aircraft would cover each other's blind spots to counter enemy fighters, outmaneuvering and engaging opposing fighters effectively by finding organized compositions in the disorderly. The maneuver typically consisted of two planes flying in a staggered formation, with one aircraft leading and the other trailing behind and slightly to the side. This tactic highlighted Claire Lee Chennault's values and principles as he would firmly emphasize the importance of teamwork and coordinated attacks among pilots, where multiple aircraft would work together to overwhelm and outmaneuver enemy formations.

In the midst of planning his strategies, Chennault did face challenges when training his pilots. Unlike the Fourteenth Air Force, where most pilots were seasoned and knowledgeable flyers, the Flying Tigers was a volunteer group, meaning many of the members were inexperienced in the field of aerial combat. However, Chennault navigated the disadvantages, introducing helpful staff jobs to members unsuitable for the air and ensuring he always had a reserve squadron at disposal. Seeing that the unit had no ranks, there was no division between the pilots and staff workers under his leadership.

THE FLYING TIGERS' LEGACY

The legacy of the AVG has spread immensely since their activation and is now widely known and appreciated throughout both China and the United States. Their story has become a fundamental part of many Chinese people's understanding of the United States. Seeing their pilots' collaboration has brought them great inspiration.

Continued appreciation for the actions of the Flying Tigers is being carried on by multiple institutions and associations in both China and the United States. For instance, the fervent Sino-American Aviation Heritage Foundation prides itself on commemorating the legacy of those who fought for and defended the skies of China.

Some of the Flying Tigers' most noteworthy accomplishments include shooting down a significant number of Japanese aircraft and disrupting Japanese air operations and plans. In particular, the Flying Tigers are credited to have shot down approximately 295-300 Japanese planes.

THE AVG AND THE FOURTEENTH AIR FORCE

While both the AVG and the Fourteenth Air Force were established in part to aid China in their fight against Japan, their primary goals differed. The Flying Tigers sought to free China from the Japanese forces who had seized control of the transportation system, effectively isolating China's Nationalist government from the rest of the world. In contrast, the Fourteenth Air Force's main objective was to ensure that China remained with the Allied Powers, assisting the United States on their grounds while the Fourteenth Air Force assisted Chinese military forces.

Progressing forward, the Fourteenth Air Force, based in Kunming, faced similar adversities as the Flying Tigers while fighting off military forces from Japan during World War II. In the early days, the Fourteenth Air Force faced numerous challenges, including logistical constraints, limited resources, and harsh operating conditions in the rugged terrain of China and Burma. Despite the obstacles before them, the Fourteenth Air Force quickly adapted to its environment and began conducting reconnaissance expeditions, blocking enemy supply lines and providing close air support to ground forces. The unit's pilots utilized their experience and expertise from past challenges and also incorporated new innovative tactics, furthering their resilience as they continued to embark on their missions.

With Japan's increasing aggression in East Asia and its invasion of China, the United States recognized the strategic importance of maintaining a strong air presence in the area to counter the Japanese' violent advances. The Fourteenth Air Force's operations frequently involved disrupting Japanese supply lines, supporting ground troops, and defending critical infrastructure in China and neighboring regions. The air force was primarily tasked with providing offense and defense against Japanese aggression as well as guarding the supply route over the Himalayan Mountains.

One instance where The Fourteenth Air Force displayed their determination to dampen the Japanese forces is the incident of the Nandu River Iron Bridge. The bridge, also known as the Devil's Iron Bridge or Old Iron Bridge, is located in the north of Hainan Province, China. It was originally built by the Japanese Imperial Army and named the Lu Palace Bridge to provide access to the land across the large river. It was the first bridge ever built over the Nandu river, yet it was bombed by the 90th Air Force's bomber crew in April 1945 to slow down Japanese troops. The bombing of the bridge was successful, however, the collapse was unsightly, and caused the future of China some issues in rebuilding and repairing the bridge.

JOBS AND OPERATION

Other than bomber groups, air forces also comprise a diverse array of air crafts and units. The Fourteenth Air Force, and many other air forces, included fighter squadrons, reconnaissance units, and maintenance. Despite being plagued by harsh weather conditions, the Fourteenth Air Force would obtain and transport their weapons through a combination of manufacturing and supply channels. Their main weapons were bombs, which were produced and manufactured in Allied bomb production facilities, primarily located in the United States. These facilities produced a wide range of bomb types, including general-purpose bombs, fragmentation bombs, and specialized munitions which were also utilized by the air force.

Bombs were stored and handled at depots, airfields, and supply points in the CBI Theater. Military personnel responsible for the operations ensured that bombs were properly stored and maintained to support operational requirements, and followed strict procedures to guarantee safety during loading and arming operations.

To further ascertain the pilots' safety in the dangerous sky, regular maintenance tasks were performed on aircraft. The planes had to be prepared to fly and be used for combat in the air; these preparations included inspecting the plane, lubricating and cleaning the gears, and minor repairs to address wear and tear and prevent mechanical failures. For consistent optimal performances and to conserve punctuality, aircraft underwent scheduled inspections and examinations at specified intervals.

These inspections, such as pre-flight, post-flight, daily, weekly, and periodic inspections, were conducted by trained maintenance technicians who could swiftly diagnose problems and replace faulty components as needed to restore them to operational status. To minimize downtime in the event of unexpected mechanical malfunctions or damage incurred in the middle of an undertaking, aircraft maintenance would be conducted right away.

During missions, pilots would begin early in the morning to load cargo and scout the Himalayan mountains for Japanese aircraft or strange changes in weather. The Fourteenth Air Force, like other air forces, tracked levels of altitude information, which helped pilots navigate and maintain proper flight paths, especially during flights over the mountainous terrain or in harsh weather conditions.

These harsh conditions made radio communication essential for coordinating air operations, receiving intelligence reports, and maintaining contact with subordinate units. Pilots, ground crews, and command centers used radios to exchange information and coordinate their activities in real-time. On more hazardous days or during ambushes from opposing forces, there were receivers that sent automatic warnings to camps and squadrons. Weather and air conditions were also within those reports. However, on better days when the sun would shine brighter than usual, pilots enjoyed taking photos to capture the momentary stillness.

Among the multitude of jobs and the perilousness of each, the members who fought in the air forces during World War I and World War II were paid a fairly high wage. As there were no ranks, every member of the Flying Tigers was paid roughly 600 USD per month by the Chinese government. Within the Fourteenth Air Force, seeing that it was a formal air force under the U.S. Army Air Corps, the pay depended on the ranks. Paid by the U.S. government, the salary for the Fourteenth Air Force pilots ranged from approximately 100 USD to 250 USD per month.

POST-WAR YEARS

As the years of World War II came to an end, the global landscape underwent many transformations, marking the beginning of a new era in international relations, politics, and society. The war incurred a tremendous human cost, with tens millions of lives lost and countless others injured or crippled for life. The end of the war brought both mourning and relief for those who had experienced the horrors of the battlefield, as well as the challenges of rebuilding shattered societies.

Countries around the world faced the task of post-war reconstruction, undergoing the process of rebuilding cities, repairing damaged infrastructure, and providing aid and support to displaced populations. The emergence of the United States and the Soviet Union as superpowers, along with the decline of European colonial powers, also reshaped the balance of power in international politics.

Some pilots continued their military careers, while others attended college or university to earn degrees in fields such as aviation, engineering, business, and various other disciplines. Similar to when Chennault retired from the U.S. Army Air Corps, some pilots decided to use the skills they gained during military service to take on public service roles such as government positions, law enforcement, or firefighting. However, many older veterans who worked for previous air forces or military divisions chose to retire and enjoy civilian life.

The end of World War II left lasting legacies in the world, shaping the collective memory of generations and influencing cultural, political, and social narratives. Memorials, museums, and commemorations dedicated to the Flying Tigers and the Fourteenth Air Force serve as reminders of the sacrifices made and the importance of preserving peace.

飛虎隊

一九四三年三月五日成軍的美國陸軍第十四航空隊，是二次大戰期間為了抵禦日本侵略而組建的部隊。這支部隊在盟軍於中緬印戰區對抗軸心國的戰事中，發揮了至為重要的作用，是扭轉戰局的一支關鍵武力。十四航空隊由一群經驗豐富的飛行員組成，當中不少人是參加過大戰其他戰區的老兵。不過在十四航空隊成軍之前，另有一支由大約三百名飛行員組成的志願隊，稱為中華民國空軍美籍志願大隊 (American Volunteer Group)。

美籍志願大隊於一九四一年投入作戰，於隔年解散，隨後許多原美籍志願隊的人員，被吸收進一九四三年成軍的第十四航空隊，由陳納德少將指揮。

美籍志願大隊的飛機因其外表塗裝而十分顯眼：每一架飛機的機鼻均採獨特的鯊魚頭塗裝。塗繪鯊魚尖牙是一種威嚇策略，用意在於使飛機更具攻擊性與侵略性；鯊魚頭塗裝也是快速辨別的有效方法，使作戰飛機在混亂的空戰中能很快辨識友機與敵機。但最重要的是，鯊魚頭塗裝使志願大隊的飛行員產生了患難與共的情誼，它是團結與榮耀的象徵。這種獨特的塗裝，也為美籍志願大隊贏得了「飛虎隊」的稱號。

陳納德將軍

陳納德無疑是飛虎隊和之後第十四航空隊的傑出領導者。他從年輕時就展現出飛行天賦，並於一九一七年加入陸軍航空隊服役，並在一次大戰期間學習飛行。在中日戰爭爆發後，陳納德受邀來到中國，希望能協助中國及其他盟國對抗日本。

在組建第十四航空隊之前，陳納德已經因在空戰方面的專業知識而備受尊重；他在華效力期間，取得許多勝利。身為飛虎隊的創始者與領導人，陳納德以善於統御和戰術創新而聞名。他強調進攻戰術、靈活變通，並重視與中國軍隊的合作，這些特質都為飛虎隊的成功做出重大貢獻。

尤其，陳納德還提倡防禦策略，也就是防止飛行員遭受不必要傷害的戰術。在他看來，這些防身策略和空戰技巧同樣重要。他力主在空戰時使用「打帶跑」（hit-and-run）戰術：從高空俯衝攻擊敵機，然後迅速爬升躲避反擊。這種戰術使得飛虎隊能妥善發揮飛機的速度與火力，同時最大程度的避免自身暴露在敵機的火力攻擊之下。

飛虎隊還採用「薩奇剪」（Thach Weave Maneuver）空戰技巧，這種空中戰術旨在對付日本先進的「零式」戰鬥機。（譯按：「薩奇剪」為美國海軍飛行員約翰・薩奇〔John Thach〕創發的空中纏鬥戰術。）這種戰術透過在混亂無序的戰場中有效組織編隊，發揚機動性，與敵機纏鬥，並能確保兩架飛機交互掩護彼此的盲點，以對抗敵軍戰鬥機。「薩奇剪」機動戰術通常以兩架飛機交錯編隊飛行，其中一架飛機在前，另一架在後面並稍微偏向一側。本戰術突顯出陳納德強調的價值觀與原則，因為他向來重視飛行員之間相互合作與協調攻擊的重要性，也就是多架飛機協同作戰，以機動性壓制敵軍機群。

在制定空戰策略的過程中，陳納德在訓練飛行員時確實面臨挑戰。飛虎隊與第十四航空隊的大多數經驗充足、本職學能豐富的飛行員不同，前者是一個志願來華參戰的團體，這表示許多成員缺乏空戰纏鬥經驗。然而，陳納德設法克服了這些不利情況，他將不適合升空作戰的隊員轉調參謀工作，得以對團體繼續提供幫助，並確保他始終擁有一支後備中隊人員可供使用。由於飛虎隊沒有軍銜，他麾下的飛行員與參謀幕僚之間也沒有任何組織區別。

飛虎隊的影響

自成軍以來，飛虎隊便廣泛傳播其影響力，其名聲現已在中、美兩國廣為人知並受到肯定。他們的故事已成為許多中國人了解美國的必備知識。戰時兩國飛行員的合作，使當今的人們深受鼓舞。

中國和美國有多個機關和團體如今仍持續舉辦紀念飛虎隊的活動。例如，熱心活躍的中美航空遺產基金會（Sino-American Aviation Heritage

Foundation），便以紀念那些為保衛中國領空而奮戰的前輩所留下的遺緒而感到自豪。

在飛虎隊最值得稱道的諸多成就之中，包括擊落大量日本飛機並破壞日軍的空軍作戰計劃。其中，飛虎隊很可能擊落了約二九五至三百架日本飛機。

飛虎隊與第十四航空隊

雖說美籍志願大隊和之後的第十四航空隊成軍的部分原因都是為了幫助中國抗日，但這兩支部隊的主要目標卻不相同。飛虎隊的作戰目標，是試圖打破日軍對國民政府統治區域的封鎖；相形之下，第十四航空隊的主要目的，是確保中國留在盟軍陣營，繼續對日作戰，協助國軍，將日軍牽制在中國戰場。

隨著局勢發展，總部位於昆明的第十四航空隊在與日本軍隊交戰時，也面臨與飛虎隊類似的困境。第十四航空隊成軍初期，面臨許多挑戰，包括後勤侷限、資源短缺以及在中緬兩國崎嶇地形中惡劣的作戰環境等。然而儘管面臨重重阻礙，第十四航空隊很快適應了環境，開始進行長程偵察任務，封鎖敵軍補給線，並向地面部隊提供近接空中支援。該部隊的飛行員利用了過去的教訓和專業知識，並採用新的空戰技巧，在繼續執行任務時增強了他們的適應力。

在日本侵略中國，並在東亞日益擴張，美國認識到在此地區駐紮強大空中武力以制衡日本攻略的戰略重要性。第十四航空隊的出擊任務，大多是阻斷日本的補給線、支援地面部隊以及保衛中國及週邊地區的關鍵基礎設施。十四航空隊的主要戰略目標是進攻日軍，並抵禦日本的侵略，同時還要保障飛越喜馬拉雅山脈的補給線。

南渡江鐵橋就是第十四航空隊決心壓制日軍進展的例證。此橋位於海南島北部，由日本皇軍興建，命名為呂宮橋，當地人則稱為「鬼子鐵橋」或「老鐵橋」。這座鐵橋是南渡江上的第一座橋樑，在一九四五年四月被美軍第九十轟炸機團攻擊，以遲滯日軍的進度。這座橋被美軍成功炸毀，但是倒塌的場面慘不忍睹，而且為中國日後重建和修復這座橋帶來了一些麻煩。

勤務與任務

除了轟炸機團之外，航空隊還編有各式各樣的飛機和單位。第十四航空隊和許多其他空軍單位一樣，也編有戰鬥機中隊、戰術偵察中隊和地勤維修單位。儘管受到惡劣天氣條件的困擾，第十四航空隊仍然透過製造和供應管道結合的方式，取得武器彈藥的補給。他們的主要武器是炸彈，在主要位於美國的盟軍炸彈廠中製造。這些兵工廠生產出多種類型的炸彈，包括一般炸彈、破片炸彈以及若干被空軍採用的特種彈藥。

這些炸彈在運送到中緬印戰區之後，在戰區的倉庫、機場和補給點進行儲存和管理。由負責軍需的地勤人員確保炸彈得到妥善儲存和維護，以因應作戰任務要求，並遵循嚴格的程序，以保障武器裝載和作戰任務期間的安全。

為求進一步保障飛行員在危機四伏的空中戰場上的安全，飛機必須進行定期維護作業。飛機要做好飛行準備，以投入空中作戰；這些準備工作包括檢查飛機、添加潤滑劑、以及清潔機組零件，同時還需進行小範圍的維修以解決組件磨損，並防止機械故障。為了始終保持飛機的最佳性能並嚴格遵守時間表，飛機均按照指定的時間進行定期維護和檢查。

這些檢查，例如飛行前、飛行後、每日、每周和定期維護，均由經過培訓的維護技術人員進行，他們可以迅速診斷問題並根據需要更換故障的零組件，以將其恢復到完善狀態。為了最大限度地減少飛機在出勤中發生意外機械故障的可能，或飛機受損後的停機時間，飛機將在出勤後立即進行維護。

在執行任務期間，飛行員會從一大早就開始裝載貨物，並在喜馬拉雅山脈中偵察日本飛機的蹤跡，或是氣候的異常變化。第十四航空隊與其他空軍部隊一樣，追蹤飛機的高度訊號，幫助飛行員導航和保持正確的飛行路徑，特別是在惡劣天候下飛越崇山峻嶺之時。

這些惡劣的條件，使得無線電通訊對於協調空中作戰、接收情報報告以及與所屬各單位保持聯繫變得極為重要。飛行員、地勤人員和指揮中心使用無線電即時交換情報並協調他們的行動。在更加危險的日子或遭到敵軍襲擊時，接收器會向營區和中隊發送自動警告。氣候和氣流狀況也在這些報告中。不過，在天氣好的時候，陽光會比平日更為耀眼，飛行員喜歡拍照來捕捉瞬間的畫面。

儘管處在繁重的工作和危險之中，飛虎隊和第十四航空隊裡參加過一次世界大戰，或曾在其他戰區服役過的老手，都領有相當高的薪酬。由於沒有軍銜，每個飛虎隊成員每月由中國政府支付約六百美元的薪餉。至於第十四航空隊，由於等同美國陸軍航空兵正規部隊，待遇是依照軍階來的。第十四航空隊飛行員的薪餉由美國政府支付，約為每月一百至二百五十美元。

戰後歲月

第二次世界大戰結束後，國際格局產生了重大的變化，國際關係、政治、社會都進入一個新的時代。這場戰爭造成了巨大的傷亡，有數千萬人喪生，無數人因戰火負傷或終身殘疾。戰爭的結束，為那些經歷過硝煙震駭、在斷瓦殘垣中面臨重建社會挑戰的人們，帶來了哀悼和寬慰。

世界各國都面臨戰後重建的任務，重建城市、修復受損的基礎建設、為流離失所的人民提供援助和支持。美國和蘇聯崛起成為超級強權，以及歐洲原殖民列強的衰落，也重塑了國際政治的權力平衡。

飛虎隊和十四航空隊的若干飛行員繼續他們的戎馬生涯，而另一些隊員則退伍進入學院，獲得航空、工程、商業和其他學門的學位。與陳納德從美國陸軍航空隊退役時類似，一些飛行員決定利用他們在服役期間學會的技能，擔任政府文職、警察或消防人員等公職。不過，也有許多曾在空軍或陸軍各部隊服役的老兵選擇退役，享受平民生活。

第二次世界大戰的結束給世界留下了持久的遺緒，塑造了幾代人的集體記憶，影響了文化、政治和社會敘事。為緬懷飛虎隊和第十四航空隊的紀念碑、博物館和紀念活動，在在提醒人們，前人所付出的犧牲和維護和平的重要性。

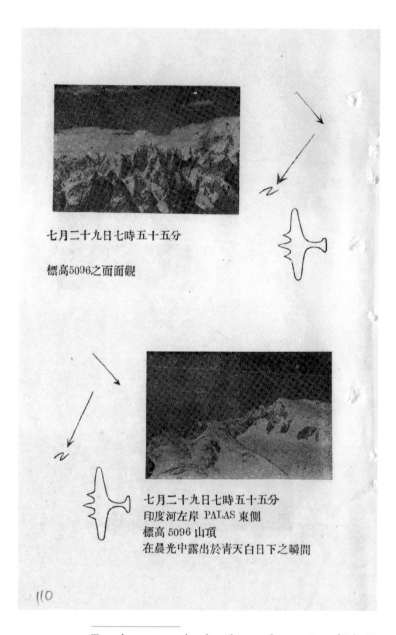

七月二十九日七時五十五分

標高5096之面面觀

七月二十九日七時五十五分
印度河左岸 PALAS 東側
標高 5096 山頂
在晨光中露出於青天白日下之瞬間

110

Two photos were taken by pilots on the morning of July 29
at an elevation level of 5096 above the mountains and the
Indus River.

七月二十九日上午，飛行員在印度河左岸東側、海
拔五〇九六英尺的山脈上方拍攝了兩張照片。

典藏號 Archive No.：020-011906-0012

圖片：國史館 photo courtesy of Academia Historica

American soldiers instruct Chinese soldiers to unload various types of bombs at an advanced airport in China.

美軍士兵指導中國士兵在中國一處前線機場卸下各類炸彈。

The Flying Tigers rush toward their aircrafts, preparing to launch a raid on a military base in Japan.

飛虎隊飛行員奔向他們的飛機，準備對日軍一處基地發動攻擊。

圖片：美國國家檔案館 photo courtesy of National Archives

General Chennault organizing documents from the U.S. Army Air Corps.

正在整理陸軍航空兵內部公文的陳納德將軍。

On April 5, 1943, Chennault received a reward
for his work in China.

一九四三年四月五日，陳納德因為在中國
服務而接受勳章。

　　　　　　圖片：美國國家檔案館 photo courtesy of National Archives

On April 10, 1945, an aircraft from the 90th Air Force bombed the Nandu River Iron Bridge, also known as the Old Iron Bridge and originally the Lu Palace Bridge.

一九四五年四月十日，美軍第九十轟炸團的一架轟炸機炸毀了原稱呂宮橋的南渡河鐵橋（又稱老鐵橋）。

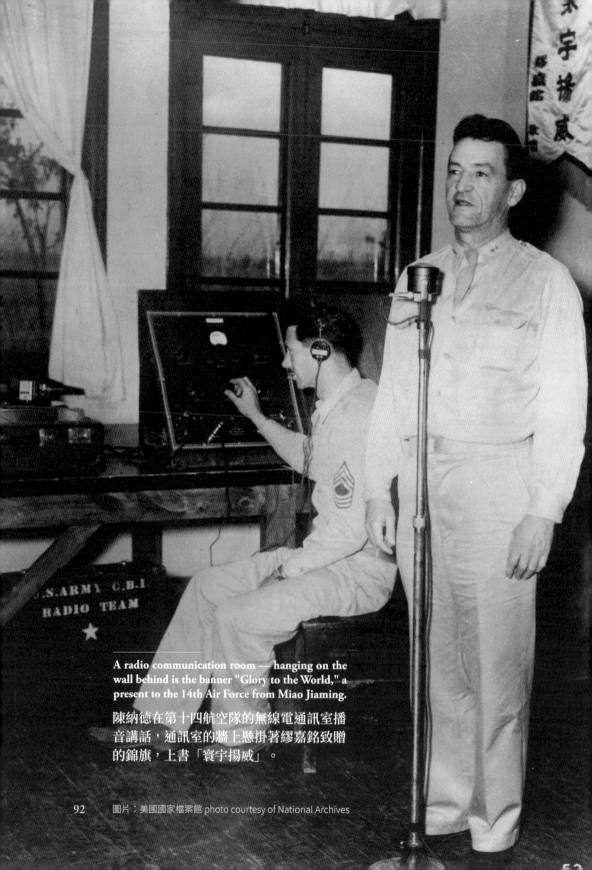

A radio communication room — hanging on the wall behind is the banner "Glory to the World," a present to the 14th Air Force from Miao Jiaming.

陳納德在第十四航空隊的無線電通訊室播音講話,通訊室的牆上懸掛著繆嘉銘致贈的錦旗,上書「寰宇揚威」。

圖片:美國國家檔案館 photo courtesy of National Archives

The Flying Tigers pilots frequently worked together to maintain and restore their aircrafts.

飛虎隊的飛行員們經常一起維修他們的飛機。

Several Chinese workers enjoyed watching aircrafts land on the runway of aircraft repair shops, affiliated with the U.S. Army Air Corps.

幾名中國民工在第十四航空隊所屬地勤維修站跑道旁觀看一架飛機降落。

圖片：美國國家檔案館 photo courtesy of National Archives

In 1944, during the break in the battle in Burma, Chinese and American soldiers flew over The Hump Route together.

一九四四年，緬甸戰事稍歇期間，中、美兩國的士兵搭機飛越駝峰航線。

An American soldier unloading gasoline while dismantling a C-87 transport aircraft.

一名美軍士兵拆卸一架 C-87 運輸機的機體，以卸載飛機裝運的汽油。

圖片：美國國家檔案館 photo courtesy of National Archives

American soldiers familiarize themselves with each other upon their arrival in China.

美軍士兵抵達中國後彼此攀談、相互結識。

Pilots and maintenance crew uninstall devices
from an aircraft after aerial combat.

一場空戰結束後，飛行員和維修人員一齊
動手，從飛機上卸下設備。

　　　　　圖片：美國國家檔案館 photo courtesy of National Archives

Members of the 14th Air Force work together to assemble a welding truck.

第十四航空隊的地勤人員正在焊接組裝一輛卡車。

圖片：美國國家檔案館 photo courtesy of National Archives

The Flying Tigers and 14th Air Force stored large bombs in designated bomb storages or depots, typically located within their airbases.

飛虎隊和第十四航空隊將大型炸彈存放在指定的彈藥庫或倉庫中,這些庫房通常位於其空軍基地內。

THE WAY
OF LIFE

The Fourteenth Air Force was deployed from the United States to China on March 5, 1943. The main objective was to ensure China's alliance with the Allied powers, given the country's critical role in supporting their war against the Axis powers. Following the China-Burma-India (CBI) Theater, the Fourteenth Air Force flew the dangerous 500-mile air route over the Himalayas — The Hump — to transport the supplies that aided China in surviving the onslaught of Japanese aggression.

INTERMINGLING OF CULTURES

Interactions between the Chinese and Americans in China were not limited, due to the fact that there were many Chinese construction workers on plane runway sites. Relations were generally cordial despite the culture shock that often struck both groups.

Although beer and alcohol was expensive to import from abroad, members of the Fourteenth Air Force were still able to enjoy their leisure time: they engaged in various sports such as playing baseball or basketball, explored local markets, visited historical sites, enjoyed local cuisine, and socialized with fellow servicemen. Some also pursued hobbies that helped them grow familiar with the foreign land and people, like photography and learning the Chinese language.

Even despite their hardships, Chinese communities and individuals offered assistance to displaced refugees and victims of war atrocities. They welcomed those in need into their homes, churches, and community centers, often providing shelter or medical care for downed American pilots as well. To protect the Fourteenth Air Force from capture by Japanese forces, they hid crewmen and pilots in barns and remote locations, risking their own safety. They rarely hesitated to tend to wounds, nursing the injured back to health and providing reassurance to the pilots during their recovery.

ENVIRONMENTAL LIVING CONDITIONS

While transporting supplies to China from the CBI Theater, the Fourteenth Air Force frequently faced difficult environmental conditions. In cases involving hazardous weather, the flight routes were diverted to the north. The extra flying time served to delay the impact of the delivery of crucial supplies over The Hump route to the Chinese Nationalist government located in Chongqing. The primary load for The Hump was gasoline, which was the fuel that helped to carry up to 55-gallon drums through the air. Loads carried over The Hump, therefore, were varied. Different materials were utilized to carry different loads of varying size and capacity.

Living standards on the ground were putrid. In fact, the typical shelters were tents or bamboo bashas, with tent foundations and sidewalks that had to be elevated to stay above standing water. Malaria and dysentery were common.

Exposed to the blistering temperatures, uniforms and boots became susceptible to mildew within a matter of days, rendering them uncomfortable and unsafe. The food provided were government-issued C-rations — canned food that could conveniently be eaten cold and uncooked — but their deficient nutritional value often left soldiers lacking in nourishment. While there were plenty of sources of water, it was frequently contaminated with bacteria and parasites.

INDUSTRIAL AND INTERNAL RELATIONS

Before the Second Sino-Japanese War in 1937, the Chinese economy was predominantly agrarian, with the majority of the population engaging in farming. While there were still pockets of industrial activity, China's industrial sector was relatively underdeveloped compared to Western countries and Japan.

The relationship between the Chinese Nationalist government and the Fourteenth Air Force during World War II was characterized by cooperation — unlike that between the Nationalists and the Communists, whose collaboration to resist Japanese aggression was fraught with tension.

THE FOURTEENTH AIR FORCE'S LEGACY

The presence of American pilots in China fostered cultural exchange and friendship between the United States and the Chinese. The Fourteenth Air Force became symbols of cooperation and solidarity between the two nations, as the unit forged strong bonds that endured beyond the war.

Located in Zhijiang, Hunan Province, China, a Flying Tigers Memorial commemorates the service and sacrifice of the American Volunteer Group (AVG). Another more unique monument is the Flying Tigers Heritage Park located in Kissimmee, Florida, USA, which pays tribute to the men and women of the Flying Tigers and the Fourteenth Air Force.

In essence, the legacy of the Fourteenth Air Force serves as an inspiration for the new generations today. The unit's determination and teamwork during their mission will continue to be respected, and their contributions during World War II are still celebrated to this day, with hopes that their legacy endures far into the future.

戰時生活

美軍航空兵第十四航空隊於一九四三年三月五日在中國成軍。有鑑於中國在對抗軸心國、與盟國並肩作戰方面發揮關鍵作用,因此第十四航空隊成軍的主要作戰目標即是保障中國與盟國結盟共同作戰。繼中緬印戰區之後,十四航空隊飛越喜馬拉雅山脈,在長達五百英里的危險航線——「駝峰」上運送物資,幫助中國抵抗日本侵略。

文化融合

由於修築機場跑道時有許多中國民工參與,中國人與美國人之間的互動交流所在多有。儘管在華美軍和與他們接觸的中國人這兩個群體之間經常出現文化衝擊,不過總的來說雙方的關係還是很融洽的。

儘管從國外進口啤酒和其他酒類代價不菲,第十四航空隊的官兵們仍然能夠享受休假時的閒暇時光:他們從事各種運動,例如打棒球或籃球比賽,探索當地市集,造訪名勝古蹟,品嚐在地美食,並與袍澤聯誼往來。有些駐華美軍官兵也培養一些的嗜好,例如攝影和學習中文,有助於他們熟悉這塊異國的土地和人民。

儘管自身也處在困境之中,中國民眾還是向流離失所的難民和日軍暴行的受害者提供援助。他們將有需要的人迎進居所、教堂和社區中心,通常也為被擊落的美國飛行員提供庇護或醫療協助。為了保護第十四航空隊的飛行員不被日軍俘虜,他們冒著生命危險,將機組人員藏匿在穀倉和偏遠地區。他們毫不猶豫地處理傷口,照顧傷患,並在康復過程中為負傷的飛行員提供撫慰與關懷。

居住環境條件

從中緬印戰區運送物資到中國,第十四航空隊經常遭遇到不少艱困的環境。倘若遇上惡劣天候,飛行航線將改向北邊。因航線北移而多出的飛行時間,有助於緩衝重要物資延遲運補到位於重慶的中國國民政府所造成的衝擊。駝峰航線主要以汽油為燃料,這種燃料能夠運送重達五十五加侖（約等於二〇八點一九公升）的圓桶升空。因此，駝峰航線載運的負荷量各不相同。在乘載各種大小與容量的物資時，運用不同的材質進行裝載。

地面生活環境十分惡劣。實際上，官兵們賴以居住、遮風避雨的營舍，幾乎都是帳篷和茅草屋，而營舍的地基和通道都必須以竹枝架高，避免浸泡在積水之中。瘧疾和痢疾也相當常見。

官兵的制服和軍靴由於長期暴露在高溫潮濕的環境下，幾天的時間就會發霉，使它們變得不舒適也不衛生。部隊的主食是美軍配發的「C」口糧（C-rations），這是罐頭預製的食品，無須加熱烹煮即可食用，相當便利，但是由於缺乏營養價值，常導致官兵營養不良。水源雖然相當充足，不過經常遭到細菌和寄生蟲的汙染。

產業與內部關係

在一九三七年中日戰爭爆發前，中國經濟以農業為主，大部分人口從事農業。儘管仍有少量工業活動，但與西方國家和日本相比，中國的工業部門相對落後。

二次大戰期間，國民政府與第十四航空隊的關係以合作為主，和國民黨與中共之間，雖然合作抗日，卻充滿緊張的關係大不相同。

第十四航空隊的遺緒

美國飛行員來華助戰，促進了中、美兩國之間的文化交流和友誼。第十四航空隊成為兩國合作與團結的象徵，也是戰後長期連結兩國邦誼的牢固紐帶。

在中國湖南省芷江市，豎立了飛虎隊的紀念碑，緬懷美籍志願大隊來華助戰的犧牲奉獻。另一個更為獨特的紀念設施，位於美國佛羅里達州基西米市（Kissimmee），名為「飛虎隊紀念公園」（Flying Tigers

Heritage Park），向飛虎隊與第十四航空隊的男女軍人致敬。

　　根本上來說，第十四航空隊啟發了當今的新世代。這支部隊在執行任務期間的決心和團隊合作將繼續受到後世的敬重，他們在第二次世界大戰期間做出的貢獻至今仍被紀念，希望他們的影響能夠綿延久遠。

An airfield runway

一處機場的起降跑道

A bird's-eye view of an airfield runway

機場跑道的鳥瞰攝影

　　　　　圖片：美國國家檔案館 photo courtesy of National Archives

In an undisclosed location in China, a water buffalo is pulling a cart across an airfield where Chinese workers are constructing aprons for U.S. Army twin-engine planes. Overhead, a U.S. Army aircraft is gearing down for landing. This scene strikingly contrasts ancient and modern modes of transportation.

在中國的一處地點保密的機場，一頭水牛正在拉著一輛大車穿過一條跑道，中國民工正在為美國陸軍雙引擎飛機建造停機坪。頭頂上，一架美國陸軍飛機正在減速準備降落。這一幕將傳統和現代的交通方式構成了鮮明的對比。

American engineers are constructing a fuel storage tank, capable of holding 500 barrels of oil, at an airfield. It is part of the China-India Oil Pipeline Project.

美國工程師正在機場建造一個可容納五百桶石油的燃料儲存槽。這是中印石油輸油管計畫的一部分。

　圖片：美國國家檔案館 photo courtesy of National Archives

U.S. Army service personnel are maintaining pipelines at an airfield.

美軍地勤人員正在一處機場維護輸送管線。

圖片：美國國家檔案館 photo courtesy of National Archives

Hundreds of Chinese workers are pulling a huge stone roller back and forth to compact and level the gravel-paved runway during the construction of a U.S. Army airfield. This photo was taken on March 31, 1944.

在建造美軍機場過程中，數百名中國工人正來回拉動巨大的石製壓路機，壓實並平整由碎石鋪成的跑道。這張照片拍攝於一九四四年三月三十一日。

圖片：美國國家檔案館 photo courtesy of National Archives

The lack of modern mechanical equipment did not hinder the ingenuity of Chinese workers in constructing airfields for the U.S. Army 14th Air Force. A Chinese boy is gathering stones and placing them in a wicker winnower. These stones are raw materials for paving the airfield runway. Around 300 children are involved in the construction of this airfield.

缺乏現代化機械設備並沒有妨礙心靈手巧的中國民工為美國陸軍第十四航空隊建造機場。一名中國少年正在收集石頭並將它們放入柳條編成的畚箕中。這些石頭是鋪設機場跑道的材料。大約有三百名兒童參與了該機場的建設。

Chinese workers are laying the foundation for the construction of a new airfield.

中國民工正在鋪設一處新機場的地基。

　　　圖片：美國國家檔案館 photo courtesy of National Archives

This photo, taken on June 26, 1944, captures women joining the workforce constructing airfields, using hammers to break large stones into small gravels. Within just three months, at least 43,000 Chinese workers are involved in constructing airfield runaways for the B-29 bombers. On January 15, 1944, U.S. Army B-29 Superfortress bombers are gearing up for strikes against the Japanese mainland.

這張照片拍攝於一九四四年六月二十六日，捕捉了婦女們加入建造機場大隊人馬，用錘子將大石頭打碎成小礫石的情景。短短三個月內，至少有四萬三千名中國民工參與了 B-29 轟炸機機場跑道的建設。一九四四年一月十五日，美國陸軍航空隊 B-29「超級堡壘」轟炸機正準備對日本本土發動攻擊。

Chinese workers are using ancient methods to construct a modern airfield. They transport slurry to the construction site using shoulder poles and wooden barrels, mixing it with crushed stones to pave the airfield runway. Under the supervision of both Chinese and American engineers, 300,000 Chinese workers are involved in the construction of the airfield.

中國民工使用古老的方法建造現代的機場。他們用扁擔和木桶將泥漿運送到建築工地，與碎石混合以鋪設機場跑道。在中、美兩國工程師的共同監督下，有三十萬名中國工人參與了機場的建設。

　　　圖片：美國國家檔案館 photo courtesy of National Archives

Without modern mechanical equipment, Chinese workers manually spread stones to lay the foundation for the airfield runway.

在缺乏現代化機械設備的情況下，中國民工以手工鋪石，為機場跑道鋪設地基。

Chinese soldiers and workers are pulling a stone roller as they
construct an airfield for the U.S. Army 14th Air Force. Despite
the lack of modern mechanical equipment, they have remarkably
completed what seemed like an impossible project.

中國士兵和工人正在拉運巨石壓路機為美軍第十四航
空隊建造機場。雖然缺乏現代化的機械設備，他們仍
然出色地完成了這項看似不可能的任務。

　圖片：美國國家檔案館 photo courtesy of National Archives

Three Chinese workers are carrying a large
wooden barrel to deliver meals to the airfield
construction site.

三名中國民工抬著一具裝滿米飯的大竹
桶，往修建機場的工地送餐。

Chinese workers are employing ancient tools like hoes, and wooden stakes to construct the airfield runway for the U.S. Army 14th Air Force.

中國民工使用鋤頭和木樁等傳統工具為美國陸軍第十四航空隊建造機場跑道。

圖片：美國國家檔案館 photo courtesy of National Archives

This photo, taken on April 6, 1944, shows that Chinese workers are moving big stones by passing them from one person to the next by hand, forming a "conveyor belt" at a U.S. airfield construction site.

這張照片攝於一九四四年四月六日，圖中民工們正用徒手接力的方式搬運用作機場建材的石頭。

Chinese workers haul large rocks from nearby hills using rubber-tired carts and stack them at the airfield construction site.

中國民工用橡膠輪胎推車從附近的山上搬來大塊岩石，然後堆放在機場施工現場。

P-43 in service with the Chinese Air Force in Kunming Airport, China on September 18, 1942.

一九四二年九月十八日，於昆明機場待命的中國空軍 P-43 驅逐機。

On September 15, 1944, soldiers of the Fifth Army took a C47 transport plane from Yunnan Station to Baoshan, China.

一九四四年九月十五日，國軍第五軍士兵搭乘 C-47 運輸機從雲南驛機場前往保山。

U.S. AIRMEN BATTLE JAPANESE IN CHINA
Members of a U.S. ground crew refill magazines with .50 caliber
cartridges while perched atop a fighter plane wing stationed
at an airfield "somewhere in China". The China Air Task Force

At an airport in China, U.S. ground crews
are filling a bomber magazine with 50-caliber
bullets.

在中國的一處機場，美軍地勤人員正在為
轟炸機彈匣裝滿五〇口徑的子彈。

General Chennault and the pilots of American
Volunteer Group.

陳納德與美國空軍援華

A Chinese soldier takes a photo with a B-29
bomber.

一名中國士兵與 B-29 轟炸機合影

In Tengchong, Yunnan, Colonel Donald L. Davis and Staff Sergeant Charles Evans are preparing to take off for combat.

在雲南騰衝，唐納德・戴維斯上校和查爾斯・艾文斯士官長正準備升空作戰。

圖片：美國國家檔案館 photo courtesy of National Archives

Several rescue crew members from the Chinese
Air Force Command have a lively conversation
with American air crewmen after work.

幾名隸屬中國空軍司令部的救援人員，在
結束執勤後與美國機組人員熱絡交談。

A display photo of an Air Force Staff Officer

一名航空兵將領的肖像。

Soldiers and air crewmen often utilized animals to assist them in transporting equipment and baggage.

官兵和機組人員經常利用動物來協助運輸設備和行李。

Chinese and American soldiers and workers traveled rugged mountain roads to transport materials and equipment.

中、美士兵和民工走過崎嶇的山路，運送物資和設備。

　　　　圖片：美國國家檔案館 photo courtesy of National Archives

**Soldiers and workers drove trucks through rocky
roads to create smooth runways.**

士兵和工人駕駛拖拉機行經崎嶇不平的路
面，以開闢平坦的跑道。

Soldiers and workers cooperate while attempting to assemble a crane.

士兵與民工齊心協力，組裝起重機吊具。

圖片：美國國家檔案館 photo courtesy of National Archives

A final check of an assembled truck's notches and grooves.

美軍士兵對一輛卡車貨廂的接榫觸及凹槽
進行最後檢查。

U.S. troops in China pose for photos with Chinese people.

在中國的美軍與中國民眾合照

圖片：美國國家檔案館 photo courtesy of National Archives

A worker packages eggs in specialized containers and crates
to protect them from damage during air transport.

一名工人將雞蛋包裝在專門的容器和板條箱中，
以確保這些雞蛋在航空運輸過程中不受損壞。

CONCLUSION

The Hump came to powerfully symbolize the bonds of friendship that characterized the war. It was an operation made possible due to the public support of Americans and the willingness of the Chinese Nationalists to accept such support and cooperation. Even if this support was comparatively lower than American efforts in other regions, it still had profound military and political implications for the Pacific and East Asia region of the world. Owing largely to the pilots of The Hump, the Allied efforts in the CBI Theater helped curtail Japanese imperial power and temporarily permitted the Nationalist Chinese to become an independent entity free of imperialist domination.

The high cost incurred by America — the number of pilots and planes lost — to fly supplies over the treacherous Himalaya mountains demonstrated the United States' will to sacrifice for China. The Chinese, in turn, showed Americans their trust and friendship when they prolonged their struggle, assuming additional responsibilities and joining the World War. Although The Hump was not without its share of initial and later difficulties, especially regarding the dangerous terrain and issues of subordination, the missions over the Himalayas from India to Yunnan as a whole were largely successfully sustained. During its operations, American planes delivered approximately 650,000 tons of supplies across the Himalayas. Moreover, President Franklin D. Roosevelt attested to the importance of The Hump by awarding The Hump carriers the Presidential Unit Citation.

The Fourteenth Air Force was one of the most important pieces related to The Hump. Emerging as one of the premier crucial Allied efforts, it was composed of highly trained pilots who would also go on to become successful in other theaters. Highlighted by the distinctive and now famous shark mouth paint scheme, this unit was only officially activated by the U.S. government in 1943. Their operations involved disrupting enemy supply lines, supporting ground troops, and protecting critical infrastructure against Japanese attacks. The Fourteenth Air Force had to overcome logistical challenges, disease, and the Japanese, challenges that required assistance from The Hump. They were vital to success in the CBI Theater and clearly demonstrate the adaptability and professionalism of the U.S.-China military operations.

The supplies delivered over The Hump were critical and helped sustain Chinese and American personnel. and pilots of The Hump constantly risked their lives to deliver supplies over the treacherous Himalayan mountains into China. Not only was the Hump technically and physically demanding, the stigma it had developed as a dangerous route also made it psychologically challenging. Many American pilots were reluctant to fly the hazardous route but did so as command believed that flying The Hump was worth the sacrifice.

The Hump prevented the Japanese from prevailing in Asia, and it catalyzed Chinese fighting spirit. It encouraged the Nationalist government of China to not only withstand the impressive military capabilities of the Japanese army, but also allowed their government to hold steady and stay together in the face of natural disaster and internal communist rebellions that threatened to overthrow Chiang Kai-shek's regime. Furthermore, it led to Allied victory during the darkest days of World War II against the Japanese. In addition, The Hump was a symbol of support for China. Its heroic delivery actions inspired soldiers, mechanics and citizens. Crucially, the bond formed between the United States and Chinese government by The Hump lasted beyond the war, although it eventually fizzled out due to the Communist takeover by the Mao Zedong.

Between 1942 and 1945, the Chinese received around 100 aircraft, and over 650,000 tons of cargo from The Hump. Brave and courageous airmen logged over 1.5 million hours of flight time. Despite The Hump's quantitative success, it also cost supplies, lives, and money. 1,314 air crewmen were killed, 468 American and 41 CNAC aircraft crashed and 81 aircraft were never accounted for. Nonetheless, The Hump's legacy should not be diminished by its casualty count. In a day and age where tensions between China and America are at an all time high, The Hump demonstrates the level of respect, cooperation, and camaraderie that the two nations once had toward each other.

The Hump also holds important lessons for handling the present Sino-American political and economic relationship. The tensions in the modern U.S.-China relationship have been on the rise, fraught with disagreements over trade policy, human rights, and foreign policy. Although this may be true, the takeaway is that cooperation during tough times or rising tensions can definitely help to boost morale of countries that require this sustained morale and control over their own affairs.

結語

駝峰航線強而有力地象徵了中、美兩國在戰爭中的友誼。由於美國朝野的鼎力支持，加上國民政府的極力配合，才得以達成這項任務。即使美國對中國的支持和援助程度，相對低於美國在其他地區的努力，但是對太平洋和東亞地區仍帶來深遠的軍事和政治影響。盟軍在中緬印戰區的作戰削弱了日本帝國的勢力，並暫時讓中華民國成為一個不受帝國主義宰制的獨立實體，在很大程度上都要歸功於駝峰航線的飛行員。

　　美國在危險的喜馬拉雅山脈上空運送物資，付出高昂代價，損失了許多飛行員和飛機，表現了美國為了支持中國所付出的犧牲。而在中國這一邊，在持久抗戰、承擔額外任務，並參與世界大戰，也向美方展現出他們對盟友的信任與友誼。雖然駝峰航線自始至終波折不斷（尤其是在危險的地勢環境與空運航線的隸屬爭議方面更是如此），但是這條從印度飛越喜馬拉雅山區、運送物資抵達雲南的任務，大致上來說還是成功的。美軍運輸機經由駝峰航線一共輸送了六十五萬噸物資。羅斯福總統也頒授「總統獎章」(Presidential Unit Citation) 給在駝峰航線服務的機組人員，肯定這條航線的重要性。

　　在與駝峰航線有關的人、事、物中，第十四航空隊是最重要的一環。這支部隊是盟軍投入亞洲戰區的重要承諾，至一九四三年才正式成軍，由訓練有素的飛行員組成（若是投入其他戰區，他們也能戰功彪炳），以機鼻獨特且著名的鯊魚嘴塗裝為醒目特色。他們的作戰任務包括阻斷日軍的補給線、支援地面部隊，以及保護重要基礎建設不受日軍的攻擊。第十四航空隊除了與日軍對抗，還必須克服後勤和疾病的種種困難。凡此種種，都需要駝峰航線的援助。駝峰航線對於盟軍在中緬印戰區的戰局勝利至關緊要，同時也清楚地顯示出中、美軍事合作因地制宜的靈活與專業態度。

　　駝峰航線運送的物資十分關鍵，能夠保障中、美人員的生命。執行駝峰航線任務的飛行員不斷冒著生命危險，翻越險惡的喜馬拉雅山脈，將物資運送到中國。駝峰航線不僅對技術和體力有很高要求，而它作為危險路線的名聲，也使這條航線對飛行員的心理上具有挑戰性。許多美國飛行員原來並不情願執飛這條危險的航線，但後來還是勉力進行了，因為指揮部認為飛駝峰航線是值得付出犧牲的。

　　駝峰航線阻止了日本帝國在亞洲的霸業，也激發中國軍民的戰鬥意志。它不但使中國國民政府能夠抵擋日本強大的軍事力量，更讓政府在面臨自然災害及圖謀推翻蔣中正政權的共黨勢力時，還可以維持穩定並團結一致。不但如此，駝峰航線更幫助盟軍度過二次大戰最黑暗的時期，最後戰勝日本。駝峰也是支持中國作戰的象徵，其英勇的行動振奮了士兵、機械技工和民眾。而最重要的是，儘管中、美關係一度因為毛澤東領導的中國共產黨席捲全國而破裂，但駝峰航線所形成維繫中、美之間的情感紐帶則一直延續到戰爭結束之後。

　　從一九四二年到一九四五年，中國方面總共經由駝峰航線，接收到約一百架飛機和超過六十五萬噸的物資。勇敢無畏的機組人員，總飛行時數超過一百五十萬小時。而縱使駝峰航線輸送的物資在數量上如此豐碩，卻也付出了生命、物資和金錢的代價。據統計，總共有一三一四位機組人員罹難，四六八架美軍運輸機與四十一架中國航空貨機失事墜毀，另有八十一架飛機下落不明。儘管如此，駝峰航線的遺澤，不應因其傷亡數字而有所減損。在當前中、美關係空前緊張之際，駝峰航線展現出昔日兩國之間曾經相互尊重、合作與友誼的程度。

　　駝峰航線對於應對當前的中、美政治與經濟關係也具有重要的教訓意義。當代美、中關係的緊張局勢不斷加劇升溫，兩國在貿易政策、人權議題和外交政策方面充滿分歧。兩國在關係惡化或緊張局勢升級期間進行合作，肯定有助於振奮各自民心士氣、並有效控管國內事務，或許這就是正確的道路。

Chinese and American soldiers unload bombs for the 14th Air Force at an advanced airport in China.

中、美士兵在中國一處前線機場為第十四航空隊卸載炸彈。

March 31, 1944: Chinese workers constructing an airport runway. They drag a huge stone roller to crush the gravel-paved runway to build the foundations of the airport.

數百名中國工人正來回拉動巨大的石製壓路機，壓實並平整由碎石鋪成的跑道。這張照片拍攝於一九四四年三月三十一日。

圖片：美國國家檔案館 photo courtesy of National Archives

Horse carriage and plane

馬車與飛機

April 15, 1945: Chinese and American generals
mourn the passing of President Franklin D.
Roosevelt. Front row from left to right: Yingqin He,
Chennault, Yun Long, McClure, Qixiang Huang.

一九四五年四月十五日，中、美兩國將領悼
念甫逝世的美國羅斯福總統。前排左至右：
何應欽、陳納德、龍雲、麥克魯、黃琪翔。

September 6, 1944: Kunming Airport, Yunnan, China. Major Mark Peace and his assistants from Y Force and the Fifth Army troops preparing to board the plane.

一九四四年九月六日，雲南昆明機場。美軍馬克・畢斯少校帶著助手們，準備和中國遠征軍第五軍士兵一同登機。

Three Chinese soldiers with a 14th Air Force pilot in the year 1944.

一九四四年，三名中國官兵與一位美軍第十四航空隊的飛行員合影。

Mitchell bombers parked at the airport being refueled to go to bomb Japan in World War II.

二次大戰期間，美軍 B-25 轟炸機正在添加燃油，準備出擊轟炸日本。

圖片：美國國家檔案館 photo courtesy of National Archives

An aerial photograph of one of the many planes
used to fly over The Hump.

一架美軍飛機正飛越駝峰航線，這是飛越
此航線眾多飛機當中的一架。

圖片：美國國家檔案館 photo courtesy of National Archives

A ground photograph of one of the many planes
used to fly The Hump.

一架飛越駝峰航線的運輸機降落時攝影。

U.S. military aircraft airdropping supplies to Chinese soldiers.

美軍飛機空投物資給國軍士兵。

圖片：美國國家檔案館 photo courtesy of National Archives

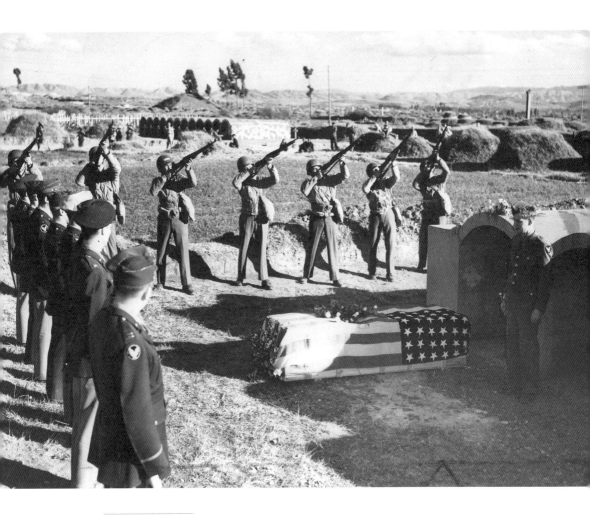

At a U.S. Air Force base in China, soldiers hold a
funeral for the sacrificed pilots.

在駐華航空基地,美軍官兵為英勇犧牲的
飛行員舉行葬禮。

In western China, Chinese and American soldiers
and civilians were packing airdrop supplies.

在華西，中、美兩國士兵及民眾正在堆放
空投物資。

圖片：美國國家檔案館 photo courtesy of National Archives

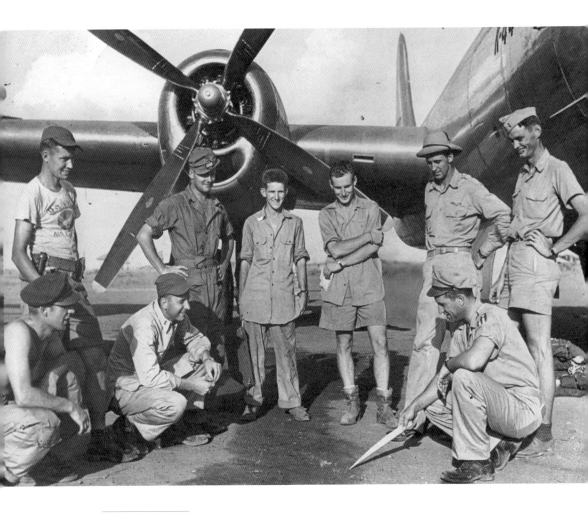

A group photo of some pilots and members of the 14th Air Force (Flying Tigers).

第十四航空隊部分隊員合影。

圖片：美國國家檔案館 photo courtesy of National Archives

Manual workers unloading and loading bombs for takeoff for The Hump.

地勤人員和搬運民工徒手裝載預備經由駝峰航線運送的炸彈。

An image captured of airdropped Hump supplies on the ground.

駝峰航線空運物資空投的場面。

圖片：美國國家檔案館 photo courtesy of National Archives

參考資料
Bibliography

Published Work 出版著作

1. Plating, John D. The Hump: America's Strategy for Keeping China in World War II. College Station, TX: A&M University Press, 2011.

2. Tunner, William H. Over the Hump (USAF Warrior Studies). Washington, D.C.: Office of Air Force History, United States Air Force, 1985, c1964.

3. King, Steven C. Flying the Hump to China. Bloomington, IN: Author House, 2004.

4. Thorne, Bliss K. The Hump: The Great Military Airlift of World War II. Philadelphia and New York: J.B. Lippincott Company, Second Printing, 1965.

5. Willett, Robert L. The Hunt for Jimmie Browne: An MIA Pilot in World War II China. Lincoln, NE: Potomac Book, 2020.

Website Data 網路資料

1. Bell Jr., Raymond E. "With Hammers & Wicker Baskets: The Construction of U.S. Army Airfields in China during World War II." Army History, no.93, Fall 2014, pp.30-54. JSTOR, https://www.jstor.org/stable/26300287.

2. Correll, John T. "Over the Hump to China." Air & Space Forces Magazine, 1 October 2009, https://www.airandspaceforces.com/article/1009hump/. Accessed 19 May 2024.

3. Dudley, Margaret. "Blackie in Burma: Pararescue…." National Museum of the Pacific War, Accessed 6 March 2024, https://www.pacificwarmuseum.org/about/news/blackie-in-burma. Accessed 19 May 2024.

4. "Claire Lee Chennault," Texas State Historical Association, https://www.tshaonline.org/handbook/entries/chennault-claire-lee, Accessed 11 April 2024.

5. "Flying the Hump | China-Burma-India: WWII's Forgotten Theater | World War II (1941-1945) | Serving: Our Voices | Veterans History Project Collection | Digital Collections." Library of Congress, https://www.loc.gov/collections/veterans-history-project-collection/serving-our-voices/world-war-ii/china-burma-india/flying-the-hump/. Accessed 19 May 2024.

6. Glines, Carroll V. "Flying the Hump." Air & Space Forces Magazine, https://www.airandspaceforces.com/article/0391hump/. Accessed 19 May 2024.

7. Hartzer, Ronald B. et al. "Leading the Way: The History of Air Force Civil Engineers 1907-2012." pp. 68-75. https://media.defense.gov/2015/Apr/02/2001329844/-1/-1/0/AFD-150402-022.pdf, Accessed 4/22/2024.

8. Lindsey, Bill. "FLYING THE HUMP DURING WORLD WAR II." Lyon Air Museum, 15 October 2020, https://lyonairmuseum.org/blog/flying-hump-during-world-war-ii/. Accessed 19 May 2024.

9. Ohl, John K. "Operation Matterhorn: Established on a shaky logistical foundation, Operation Matterhorn failed—almost before it began." Warfare History Network. November, 2006. https://warfarehistorynetwork.com/article/ operation-matterhorn/, Accessed 4/23/2024.

10. Kinyon, Jack. "Air Transport Command-Airlift During WWII." Air Mobility Command Museum Foundation. https://amcmuseum.org/history/air-transport-command-airlift-during-wwii/, Accessed 4/23/2024

11. Lindsey, Bill. "Flying the Hump During World War II." Lyon Air Museum. https://lyonair museum. org /blog/flying-hump-during-world-war-ii/#:~:text=The%20first%20 supply%20 mission%20over,25s%20of%20the%20Doolittle%20Raiders, Accessed 23 April 2024.

12. "Flying the 'Hump' Lifeline to China." National Museum of US Air Force. https:// www. national museum.af.mil/Visit/Museum-Exhibits/Fact-Sheets/Display/Article/3627010/ flying-the-hump-lifeline-to-china/, Accessed 23 April 2024.

13. "Cheng Tu Airfield." Pacific Wrecks. https://pacificwrecks.com/airfields/ china/ cheng_ tu/ index.html, Accessed 4/22/2024

14. Weidenburner, Carl W. "The Hump - LIFE - September 11, 1944." CHINA-BURMA-INDIA, https://www.cbi-theater.com/life091144/life091144.html. Accessed 19 May 2024.

15. "The Living Legacy of the Flying Tigers," The Diplomat, https://thediplomat. com/2021/07/the-living-legacy-of-the-flying-tigers/, Accessed 29 April 2024.

16. "The Hump and Burma Road." Wikipedia. https://en.m.wikipedia.org/wiki/File: The_ Hump_ and_Burma_Road.png#file, Accessed 8 April 2024.

17. Wikipedia, https://www.cherokeephoenix.org/news/we-served-thompson-served-on-b-24-bomber-during-world-war-ii/article_c4048645-0af2-5d69-b537-de746cab0a42. html. Accessed 19 May 2024.

18. Wikipedia, https://www.airuniversity.af.edu/ASPJ/Book-Reviews/Article/1192798/the-hump-americas-strategy-for-keeping-china-in-world-war-ii/. Accessed 19 May 2024.

19. Wikipedia, https://airuniversity.af.edu/ASPJ/Book-Reviews/Article/1192798/the-hump-americas-strategy-for-keeping-china-in-world-war-ii/. Accessed 19 May 2024.

20. Wikipedia, http://www.cbi-history.com/part_ii.html. Accessed 19 May 2024.

21. Wikipedia, http://www.cbi-history.com/part_vi_2nd_air_transport_sq3.html. Accessed 19 May 2024.

22. Wikipedia, http://www.faqs.org/docs/air/avc46.html. Accessed 19 May 2024.

23. "B-25D-15 "Blackie's Gang" Serial Number 41-30362." Pacific Wrecks, 9 December 2022, https://pacificwrecks.com/aircraft/b-25/41-30362.html. Accessed 19 May 2024.

24. Wikipedia, "Nandu River Iron Bridge," https://en.wikipedia.org/wiki/Nandu_River_ Iron_Bridge, Accessed 19 April 2024

歷史影像 2

飛越駝峰：圖說抗戰期間中美空中運輸

Flying the Hump: A Photographic History of Sino-American Air Transport During World War II

喆閎人文

創 辦 人 / 楊善堯
學術顧問 / 皮國立、林孝庭、劉士永

主編 Edit / 楊善堯 Yang, Shan-Yao
作者 Author / Patrick Hao（郝健坤）、Catherine Liu（劉天悅）、Ellie Wang（王寶琪）、
　　　　　　　　Everett Wang（王艾唯）、Lucas Yuan（袁浩文）
翻譯校對 Translation and proofreading / 廖彥博 Liao, Yen-Po
設計排版 Design Layout / 吳姿穎 Wu, Tzu-Ying
策畫 Collaboration / CompassPoint Mentorship

出版 Publish / 喆閎人文工作室 ZHEHONG HUMANITIES STUDIO
地址 Address / 242011 新北市新莊區中華路一段 100 號 10 樓
　　　　　　　　10F., No. 100, Sec. 1, Zhonghua Rd., Xinzhuang Dist., New Taipei City 242011 ,
　　　　　　　　Taiwan (R.O.C.)
電話 Telephone / +886-2-2277-0675
信箱 Email / zhehong100101@gmail.com
網站 Website / http://zhehong.tw/
臉書 Facebook / https://www.facebook.com/zhehong10010

初版一刷 First Edition Brush / 2024 年 6 月
定價 Pricing / 新臺幣 NT$ 350 元、美元 USD$ 12 元
ISBN / 978-986-99268-8-1
印刷 Print / 秀威資訊科技股份有限公司 Showwe Taiwan

國家圖書館出版品預行編目 (CIP) 資料

飛越駝峰：圖說抗戰期間中美空中運輸 = Flying the hump : a photographic history of Sino-Amerecan air transport during World War II / 郝健坤 (Patrick Hao), 劉天悅 (Catherine Liu), 王寶琪 (Ellie Wang), 王艾唯 (Everett Wang), 袁浩文 (Lucas Yuan) 著 . -- 初版 . -- 新北市 : 喆閱人文工作室 , 2024.06
　面 ;　公分 . -- (歷史影像 ; 2) 中英對照
ISBN 978-986-99268-8-1(平裝)

1.CST: 中日戰爭 2.CST: 軍事運輸 3.CST: 航空運輸 4.CST: 中美關係

628.58　　　　　　　　　　　　　113008440